SIMPLE MINDS
GLITTERING PRIZE

DAVE THOMAS

Omnibus Press
London/New York/Sydney/Cologne

ISBN 0.7119.0617.3
Order No OP 43231

Exclusive distributors:
BOOK SALES LIMITED
78 Newman Street, London W1P 3LA, UK.

CHERRY LANE BOOKS
PO Box 430, Port Chester,
NY 10573, USA.

OMNIBUS PRESS
GPO Box 3304, Sydney,
NSW 2001, Australia.

To the Music Trade only:

MUSIC SALES LIMITED
78 Newman Street, London W1P 3LA, UK.

Typeset by Capital Setters, London.

Printed in England by
J.B. Offset Printers (Marks Tey) Limited, Marks Tey.

I was not able to talk to Simple Minds during the
course of my research for this book, but that is not to
say that they do not have their fair say in what is,
after all, their story. For the use of quotes and
additional information, I would like to thank the
following publications; 'Melody Maker,' 'Zig Zag,'
'Record Collector,' 'Record Mirror,' 'Soundcheck,'
'No. 1,' 'New Musical Express,' 'Smash Hits' and
'Sounds,' all of whose archives have proven an
invaluable source of enlightenment; also Brian
Hogg and David Sinclair, whose fond memories of
Simple Minds' early days lent so much substance to
these pages, and Peter Doggett, Michael Cox and Jo-
Ann Greene for their assistance in compiling the
discography.

DAVE THOMAS 1985.

CONTENTS

❦

INTRODUCTION

The queue starts forming before dawn has even broken over the Glasgow skyline. A few hardy perennials down at the front have apparently been here all night, rolled up in their sleeping bags or talking quietly over a thermos flask. But for most of us, faced with a choice between a warm bed and a hard pavement, the first bus of the morning was quite early enough.

By 10 the queue disappears around the corner and threatens to delay the post-rush hour traffic by several millennium. Or so the police would have you believe as they rush around in a blur of blue, clearing the road and unblocking the pavement. You can almost hear them praying for the box office to open.

The line begins to move forward – all those prayers must have had some effect. Someone says tickets are limited to four per person. Someone else says this guy down the front is asking everybody to buy as many as they can. Nobody wonders why. An excited murmur runs down the queue like an electric current. Will there still be tickets left by the time the people at the end get there? The band are playing three nights; judging by the length of the queue they should be playing 300.

There aren't many superlatives left now.

Seven years of making music have seen Simple Minds run right through the book. Absorbing to zippy, amazing to zealous, Simple Minds have attracted them all. Their new album was straight in at number one, the last one's galloping up the chart to join it. You can't open a music paper without there being another date or two added to the current tour. Thirty odd dates, and every one a sell out. They've just come back from Australia – it was the same out there.

It hasn't always been like this, of course. It doesn't seem that long ago that Simple Minds were Johnny And The Self Abusers, screaming out the odds at anyone brash enough to drop into the Mars Bar back in '77. Then they changed their name, changed their style, and the word started to spread. By the end of '78 you had to get to the gig very early indeed if you wanted to see the band. A year after that you'd be lucky to even hear them – the doors would be locked a long time before the show started.

Then the records started to sell. Slowly at first; a mini hit there, a minor hit there. The halls started getting larger. So did the audience. By the time "Promised You A Miracle" charted, there probably wasn't a venue in all of Scotland that Simple Minds couldn't fill. Not many

anywhere else, either. It was uncanny in a way. Every time they came back, the band was bigger. The queues were longer, the black market prices were higher. Yet it would all be accomplished with the minimum of fuss. No hype, no propaganda. For nine, ten months, you wouldn't hear a word. Then, bang. Simple Minds would be back and it was as if everybody in town was out to greet them. They used to be lucky if they sold 30,000 albums. Now they sell ten times that many in Britain alone. Their walls at home must be littered with gold discs, there is barely a country in the world which hasn't given them one. And when you see Simple Minds onstage, you know why.

At the back, Mel Gayner – a walking powerhouse if ever there was one. He flails at his drums, laying down that thunderous beat; bam, bam, bam-balam. Derek Forbes standing stock still, his fingers a blur as his bass hits your stomach like a steamhammer. Charlie Burchill lets rip on his guitar, dazzling rhythms, awesome solos. Mick McNeil standing off to one side, barely visible behind his mountains of keyboards, as he builds up astonishing walls of sound. Finally Jim Kerr, coming out dancing and never letting up, not even for a second. Whirling, spinning, leaping, never fluffing a line or missing a note. Nervous energy, pent up power. Like a spring he winds up, then lets go. The music crashes forth.

They open with "Waterfront", slowly building up as Jim shouts a greeting to the rapturous crowd. Glasgow might not be the nicest place in the world, but it is one of the most loyal. I remember seeing Alex Harvey at the Apollo, in 1975. He was just beginning to break through on a national level, but by the state of the crowd you'd think it was the second coming. He pulled out all the stops that night, gave one of the greatest shows of his life, but he could just as easily have sat on the stage and picked his nose. Once the city has taken you to its heart, you stay there come hell or high water. Perhaps Jim and Charlie were at that gig, hopping off the bus from Teryglen, and forcing their way into the excited mêlée at the doors. If they were, they'll know exactly what the audience are feeling tonight.

"Up On The Catwalk", "Glittering Prize", "The American". The hits race past.

"Speed Your Love To Me", their greatest song ever. The show could go on all night. The audience would never tire. Every lyric is echoed, every chord is mimed. There are 2,000 people here who know the songs backwards. "Big Sleep", "New Gold Dream", "Love Song" . . .

Simple Minds are a phenomenon. There really is no other word for them. Quietly and subtly they built themselves up. They promised you a miracle, now they are delivering it. The glittering prize is theirs – and yours – for the taking.

SAINTS

AND SINNERS

Jim Kerr, Charlie Burchill and Brian McGee were all born within a year of each other in Glasgow, the third largest city in Britain. Glasgow is a bleakly depressing place. Buildings like the medieval cathedral – the only surviving example of its type on the Scottish mainland – and the many parks scattered throughout the city cannot hide the scars of the last century's industrial legacy.

Standing on the banks of the River Clyde, Glasgow's focal point is its waterfront. An endless parade of warehouses and factories, this was once the home of the city's fabled shipbuilding industry. Today, however, the warehouses stand empty, and the factories are idle, further victims of 20th Century recession. But with them have also gone another of Glasgow's one time features, the slum districts for which the city became notorious. Areas like the Gorbals, with their misery, poverty, and sub-

culture that was unique, are finally being cleared. Unfortunately the tower blocks and council estates which have replaced them are scarcely any better.

"It's the sort of place where being a hairdresser is about the only form of self expression. If people asked what you did and you said 'I write words' they'd say: 'Are you queer? Are you weird?'," Jim Kerr was later to say.

Jim, Charlie, and Brian met at Holyrood Catholic school in 1973. In an interview with *Record Mirror*, Jim recalled how he and Brian were introduced. A staunch David Bowie fan, Jim was impressed when McGee arrived at school with a copy of Bowie's "Ziggy Stardust" album and a Wizzard key ring.

"I said 'Where did you get that?' and he says 'I made it,' so I said 'Gonna make me a Bowie one?' And he did and he didn't skin me for it. He gave me it for nothing."

At the time Wizzard and Bowie were among the more bizarre proponents of glam rock, a musical flirtation with sexual androgyny which, in the words of the *New Musical Express'* Charles Shaar Murray, "hit rock 'n' roll like an unnaturally luminous tidal wave . . . leaving nothing but a sequinned scum over some of (what) it touched." The brute sexuality which had always been a vital ingredient in rock mutated into a fantasy world where, to paraphrase Ray Davies, boys were now girls and girls were now boys.

David Bowie, admitting "I'm gay", and Marc Bolan, whose sexual projection had never been less than ambiguous, were as adored by one sex as the other. And in their wake everybody from faded old-timers to imperious young cavaliers came bursting out of the closet. But such was the hysteria of the time that nobody once thought to ask what they had been doing in the closet in the first place. Putting away the Hoover, perhaps?

The beauty of glam rock was that it could be indulged on whatever level you chose. You could live it, you could act it, you could simply use it for a few neat promo pictures, then shut it away in the wardrobe until next time. For every Marc Bolan, there were a hundred Sweets and Muds. Their make-up and lisps were great for the show, but underneath the greasepaint there was always a picture of the Queen, just to

remind them where their true destinies lay. And for each and every band like that, there were the Rods and Eltons, grizzled old rockers quick enough to be leading, rather than riding on, the latest bandwagon. An old gold lamé jockstrap will never let you down.

Bands like Wizzard certainly fell into the latter category. Leader Roy Wood had been the driving force behind The Move, psychedelic upstarts of half a decade before. Wizzard, his early Seventies incarnation which so impressed the young McGee, was little more than a fifties revival outfit. But in blending the music of his own school days with the visual preoccupations of the new generation, Wood became as valid a contender as any more youthful outfit. He would appear on *Top Of The Pops* in a multi-hued wig, a straggling mane of green, red and blue. His mascara would be running, his face-paint a wildly applied kaleidoscope. In an age of visual

excesses, Wood left most people at the starting blocks.

For a young exhibitionist, as Jim Kerr remembers himself, these excesses provided the ideal opportunity for drawing attention to yourself. Jim remembers ". . . going to gigs dressed up in the whole Glam thing; big boots, mascara, painted nails. Next day I'd be working on my building site, trying to get enough money to go hitch-hiking round Europe, and I'd notice I'd still got a trace of nail varnish on. And I'd be terrified these giants, these bears that I worked with, would discover it. Other than that, of course, I was perfectly normal."

Jim left school in the summer of 1976, and quickly found work as an apprentice engineer.

But his heart was not in it, especially when he saw Brian McGee making just as good a living from his own parent's generosity.

Jim told *Record Mirror*: "All my mates that had always been on the level with me in the past seemed to be content and I wasn't. It wasn't as if I felt superior or anything. I felt inferior if anything. Sometimes it's a pure pain to be aware."

Jim suffered from a pronounced stutter and, according to popular legend, took up singing as much for therapy as self expression. He reasoned that if he could grow accustomed to using his voice as an instrument, it would help him overcome the nervousness which caused the impediment. So, together with Charlie Burchill, Jim and Brian decided to pool their resources into a group.

1976 was the era of punk. In London The Sex Pistols, The Damned, The Clash and The Adverts were all taking their first tentative steps into the public arena. In Manchester The Buzzcocks and Slaughter And The Dogs were doing likewise. Within six months the country was alive with their contemporaries and imitators.

The Scottish scene developed parallel to its Sassenach equivalent. The Rezillos, from Edinburgh, were the first group to make an impact on a national level. "Can't Stand My Baby", their début single, a glorious rush of comic cut adrenalin, was a regular on the independent chart for much of 1977. Behind them, Dunfermline's The Skids, Glasgow's The Exile, and Dundee's The Drive (whose label, N-R-G, was Scotland's first independent), all fought to make themselves heard.

The catalyst in the emergent scene was Bruce Findlay. He managed Bruce's Record Shop in Edinburgh, and felt proud that it was the only store in the area where people could actually buy the 'new' music. The shop's weekly fanzine, "Cripes", was *the* guide to the local punk scene, a catalogue of the shop's best selling records and the week's new releases. The shop was actually owned by the Guinness corporation but when Bruce decided to found his own record label in July 1977 and set up offices about the shop, his bosses quickly agreed to help finance the operation.

Bruce's first signing was a local band, The Valves. He went to see them on the recommendation of one of his customers. Within a week of that first meeting the band were in the

studio, cutting their first single. It was followed, shortly after, by Zoom Record's second release, a triple A-side by PVC2. When that band broke up, almost immediately after "Gonna Put You In The Picture" reached the shops, Findlay retained three quarters of the line-up as The Zones.

PVC2 had, in fact, once been known – and widely reviled – as Slik, the last of the great teenybob hopes. They surfaced in December 1975, almost a year after their first single sank without trace. "Forever And Ever", a swift chart-topper, was a cleverly constructed pop tune which had the Glaswegian quartet don American baseball outfits in an attempt to create an image that might rival The Bay City Rollers' more established tartan look.

Despite sharing the same record label – Bell/Arista – as the immensely popular Rollers, it was evident that an atmosphere of competition was being generated. But while the Rollers' reign was to continue well into the following year, Slik managed just one more hit, the monastic dirge, "Requiem". An album and two further singles all bombed. A paperback biography by GLC Tory councillor George Tremlett, the fourteenth in a series that threatened to engulf the world, was already destined for the remainder bins when it came off the printing press.

Having lost momentum there seemed little likelihood that Slik would be able to regain it, and the advent of punk reduced their chances still further. So, in spring 1977, the band's vocalist, Midge Ure, and drummer, Kenny Hyslop, set up a budget priced recording session for the band and were rewarded when the ensuing PVC2 single easily made the Top Ten in *Sounds*' New Wave chart.

These three tracks were to be PVC2's sole contribution to western culture. Midge Ure moved down to London shortly after and formed The Rich Kids with Glen Matlock, Steve New and Rusty Egan. The remaining trio recruited a new guitarist, Willy Gardner, from The Hot Valves, and changed their name to The Zones. Their first single, "Stuck With You", was Zoom Records' fourth single. It followed a second effort by The Valves, released early in 1978.

Unfortunately, despite further such essays in eloquent pop, The Zones were never to successfully deliver the goods promised by well

received gigs with the likes of The Clash and Iggy Pop. Other Zoom signings, like The Questions, Nightshift, sixties survivor Mike Heron, and the highly innovative London Zoo, fared no better, and Zoom Records was left to seek out a more inviting commercial proposition. It arrived in June 1978, with a band who rose from the ashes of Johnny And The Self Abusers.

Johnny And The Self Abusers was a seven piece outfit constructed around the nucleus of Jim Kerr, Charlie Burchill and Brian McGee. They played their first gigs in February 1977, inspired – so Kerr later claimed – by the blackness and negativity of those days. Boasting the unwieldy line-up of three guitars, bass, drums, saxophone and Kerr's harsh, undisciplined vocals (described as "an uncontrolled scream" by one Glasgow fanzine), Johnny And The Self Abusers played regularly around Glasgow. And although their allegiance to the Glasgow punk scene was given more by proxy than direct action, they quickly established themselves as one of the area's leading bands. Regular gigs at the tiny Mars Bar club won them a spreading reputation and by the summer their name was known as far south as London's Camden Town. Here stood the offices of

Chiswick Records, the label to which Johnny And The Self Abusers signed in early autumn.

Talking to *Record Mirror* three years later, Jim was to say: "Although we were in with things that were happening, what with our name and everything, we were doing stuff off Doctors of Madness albums. It was always on that level rather than singing about riots and daft things like that."

But this was not evidenced by the band's November 1977 single. Though it was plain they were making an effort to set themselves apart from the multitude of other cut and thrust punk bands, the two songs on the single, "Saints And Sinners" and "Dead Vandals", gave little indication that here were the first buddings of a great new talent.

"They have a great name," Jon Savage wrote in *Sounds*, "but the song doesn't do much. It's hard, but they're competing with dozens of other bands producing similar stuff in a wider market place which, bar a few major bands, hasn't exactly opened its arms or pockets." In the *New Musical Express*, the single was condemned as ". . . a futile thrashing of pseudopunk, Bowie colliding with Berry", while *Melody Maker* called it "relentlessly rank and file". Not an auspicious start by any means and, not surprisingly, the band felt unhappy about what they were doing.

For Jim, Charlie, and Brian, the whole exercise had been tongue in cheek, born purely out of the excitement of what was happening around them. They had little faith in what they were doing and the idea of continuing to do it was mortifying. They seldom found the opportunity to play outside of their native Glasgow and they had never made the trip across Hadrian's Wall. So, with their contracted single recorded and ready to be shipped, Johnny And The Self Abusers celebrated its release in the only way they could: By splitting up the same day that "Saints And Sinners" was released.

The biggest problem within the band was a clash of personalities between the three founder members on the one hand, and the remaining quartet on the other. Charlie Burchill later remarked, "We knew things couldn't go on any more. So finally, the unsatisfactory element left, and the good element went on to form Simple Minds."

It was the "unsatisfactory element" who made the early running. Ali Mackenzie and John Milarky lost no time in putting together Cuban Heels, and for four months solid they played clubs and pubs around Scotland. In April 1978, they released their first single, a reworking of Petula Clark's "Downtown", on the Housewive's Choice label.

Described by the *New Musical Express* as Scotland's most obscure independent, Housewive's Choice lasted for just that one single. The next time Cuban Heels surfaced, in August 1980, they were débuting the Greville label.

Neither the singles nor the band's repeated attempts at making demo tapes made any impression on the major record companies that Mackenzie tried to attract. Finally, deciding that if you can't beat them you have to join them, Mackenzie put together yet another independent company, but this time he intended doing the job properly.

Cuba Libre was intended to showcase not only Cuban Heels, but other Scottish outfits as well. The Shakin' Pyramids and The Zones' Willy Gardner were both added to the label's roster, and within a very short time the label had

achieved one of its chief objectives.

Cuban Heels' latest single, "Walk On Water", had already attracted some record company interest. When The Shakin' Pyramids took London's Venue by storm a few weeks later, Virgin Records pounced. They agreed to take over Cuba Libre's distribution and marketing, with their own logo taking pride of place over Cuba Libre's. And while the arrangement failed to produce any hit records, all parties concerned would seem to have got at least some of what they wanted.

Several years after Johnny And The Self Abusers broke up Charlie Burchill was to look back and say, "We felt that what was being pumped out in that last year was a challenge. Almost on a parallel with the boogie bands, the punks did that exact same speed of number – guaranteed to shock and get people going. And that really isn't the function of music. So much

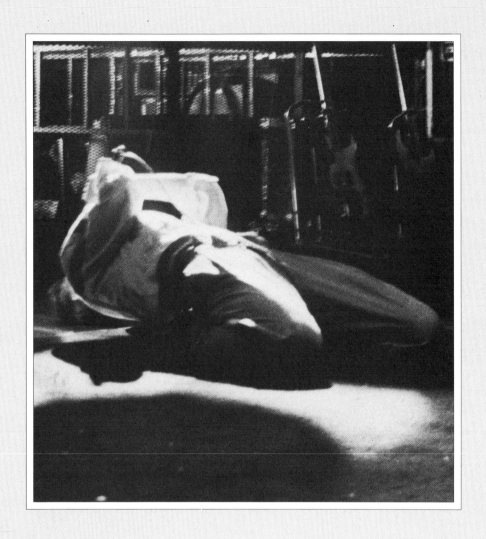

of the punk era was a political movement. It got to the stage where guys were singing about nine to five jobs and life on the dole, and it was really boring. Just saying 'I'm bored, full stop' didn't appeal to me."

"There was always an art thing in us," *Soundcheck* quoted Jim as saying. "We wanted to get a band along those lines of darkness and a sort of awareness, and put it over in an attractive type of art package. We wanted a band that could project."

Their first step was to advertise for a keyboard player – a surprising omission from Johnny And The Self Abusers' formidable arsenal of instruments. None appeared, so second guitarist Duncan Barnwell was recruited instead.

In this form Simple Minds played their first ever gig at Satellite City, a discotheque set above Glasgow's premier rock venue The Apollo. Within weeks keyboard player Mick McNeil and bassist Derek Forbes were recruited into the line-up.

The two newcomers both had interesting pasts. Forbes, a seasoned veteran of dance bands, had lately returned to Glasgow from Spain where he had been working around tourist resorts. Mick McNeil was more accustomed to the pressures of fame. At the age of nine he took up the accordion and with his brother Danny formed a band called The Barnets. They found regular work playing local dances and their Big Moment came with an appearance on the sixties TV show Junior Showtime. "I spent the next year walking around school with a very red face," Mick said later.

In May 1978, Simple Minds recorded their first demo tape. They used Savva Studios, a studio which along with the better known Barclay Towers, was the only place in town where a band could get a decent sound for a reasonable price. But unlike Barclay Towers, you didn't have to carry your gear up seven flights of stairs to do it.

The tape consisted of half a dozen songs, each one already established within their live set: "Act Of Love", "Chelsea Girl", "Wasteland", "Did You Ever", "Cocteau Twins", and "Pleasantly Disturbed". The tape was promising, if derivative. Still formulative as musicians and composers, Simple Minds were at times prone to allow influences to get the better of them, but the band's own abilities and ideas were still given plenty of opportunity to shine.

Lindsay Hutton, writing in *ZigZag* twelve months on, described the tape as "one of the greatest demos ever". Journalist Brian Hogg, who later became press agent for both Zoom Records and Simple Minds, was a little more discerning, if none the less enthusiastic. "What attracted me to Simple Minds in the first place was that they didn't really sound like anybody else. The influences were there, but you couldn't just point to them and say 'well that's so and so, that's someone else'. They had this really dense, churning, mysterious sound. That was what came over best, both on the tape and live," he said.

But the tape was to find no other takers. It was badly mixed, record companies would say. The band sounds too much like Talking Heads. Only not as good. According to Jim, "We came down to London in the July, but I felt that the companies that we got in touch with had had their fingers burned. The bands they had signed didn't seem to be taking off. I got that impression from both Polydor and CBS."

Bruce Findlay at Zoom turned them down as well, despite his having found the tape as enjoyable as any he had received. Zoom, he felt, already had a full quota of artists. There really wasn't room for any more. He was swiftly forced to recant that decision.

In August Simple Minds made their début appearance in Edinburgh, opening for Generation X at a gig promoted by one of The Cuban Heels' mentors, Steve Mackie. This show gave Brian Hogg his first exposure to the band. "When Johnny And The Self Abusers broke up, it always looked like it was going to be The Cuban Heels half that would do the best. Then one night some friends mentioned that they were going to see 'the other half of the Abusers', a band called Simple Minds. That was around January, February, but I didn't get to see the group until the Generation X gig. They were absolutely superb."

Earlier in the Seventies Brian had worked for Bruce Findlay by helping out in the shop. The two remained in touch and so the very next day Brian phoned Findlay and recommended that he go and see Simple Minds.

By the time Findlay got around to it Simple Minds had already been featured by Hogg in *Cripes*. The article, Simple Minds' first press appearance of any length, was simply a review of the gig but Hogg's enthusiasm and the band's live performance combined to persuade Findlay that Simple Minds were not only likely candidates for his Zoom label but worth taking on as managerial clients. Bruce Findlay's enthusiasm, once sparked, burned fiercely. He guided them skilfully, his direction coming not from any particular business knowledge but an all-consuming love for the band. He was, first and foremost, a fan, and today, still installed as Simple Mind's manager, he continues to be a fan.

Dave Sinclair, of London Zoo, remembers Bruce as ". . . a really manic guy, total wired up energy. He was fanatical about Simple Minds, completely devoted from the word go. He isn't your regular rock and roll entrepreneur because he has always had this genuine enthusiasm. Even in the early days, when London Zoo were playing with Simple Minds, you knew that if they were ever to make it, Bruce would be a very big factor in their doing so. And I think he has."

The courtship between Zoom and Simple Minds was to last nearly four months. Brian Hogg remembers: "First we had to persuade Simple Minds that Zoom was the right record company for them, then we had to persuade Arista that Simple Minds were the right band for Zoom.

"Arista were very twitchy, especially when they heard how much money Simple Minds wanted. It was something like full recording costs, plus a year's wage for all the band and their two permanent road crew. And on top of that, they wanted new equipment as well!

"So Arista sent Ben Edmonds, who was their head of A&R, along to see the band. Then Andrew Bailey, who was working freelance for Edmonds came along, and finally Robert White, Arista's business affairs manager. Then, when all three had reported back, saying how great they thought Simple Minds were, Charles Levison, who was the boss there, agreed to sign the band."

Robert White, in fact, was so impressed that when Bruce Findlay finally became Simple Minds' official manager in April White came in as his partner.

Under the circumstances, the record

contract was an unusual one. Though Simple Minds were technically signed to Zoom, their financial demands necessitated that they be contracted to the parent company in a separate deal to the one binding Zoom and Arista. Though nobody realised it at the time, the arrangement left Zoom at something of a disadvantage should they decide to part company with Arista before Simple Minds' own, two year, contract had expired.

A lucrative recording contract was not the only indication that Simple Minds was a band in the right place at the right time. Under the guidance of *NME* journalist and early ally Ian Cranna, and then Bruce Findlay, Simple Minds was an all but obligatory choice for support slot whenever a major band visited Scotland. Not only was Simple Minds' presence guaranteed to attract a capacity crowd quite apart from the headlining act, they were also the only Scottish outfit operating at that level who were unanimously declared capable of matching up to the headliner's own abilities. Of that there could be no doubt – especially after the band so irreverently upstaged Siouxsie And The Banshees at Glasgow Apollo after being added to the bill at just an afternoon's notice.

And for people south of the border who had yet to sample Simple Minds' magic, a review in the *New Musical Express*, in October 1978, served notice that something big was afoot.

"You know that band everybody's been waiting for – the one that will achieve that magical fusion of the verbal visions of the Bowie/Harley/Verlaine twilight academy with the fertile firepower of the New Wave, that early Roxy Music with a rock and roll heart? Well here they are."

It was an hyperbolic review – not surprising, since it had been written by Ian Cranna – but Simple Minds were an hyperbolic band. They were still less than a year old and several of their songs were left overs from the Johnny And The Self Abusers' days – "Dead Vandals", for instance. But the sheer range of their musical vision could not help but leave onlookers breathless. And there was no mistaking that Ian Cranna's words touched the very heart of Simple Minds' earliest preoccupations. When he wrote of David Bowie, Steve Harley, Tom Verlaine and Roxy Music as

ranking amongst the band's influences he was not inviting comparisons. His intentions were to inform. By pointing to territories mapped out by those artists, he was supplying readers with a few familiar landmarks to take with them when they encountered Simple Minds.

To Cranna's list could be added Van Der Graaf Generator, Sparks, The Velvet Underground (both individually and collectively), The Doctors of Madness and Brian Eno. These were artists whom *New Musical Express'* Paul Morley described as "erratically stirring darkness, disgrace and melodrama into a mixture of psychedelia, torch, cabaret and electronics, making noises that shocked and repelled."

It was these left field tendencies which would set Simple Minds apart from their contemporaries. Other bands might experiment with the outer limits of their audiences' expectations; Simple Minds were the first band to turn such dreams into reality.

THE NEW SOUND

In November Duncan Barnwell was ousted from the group. The departure was not a hasty one but it still took Bruce Findlay and Brian Hogg by surprise when Simple Minds trooped up to the office to announce that Duncan was out. The problems were solely of a musical nature. Duncan's ideas of how the band should project themselves visually and musically did not sit well with the rest of the group. For him to have remained would eventually have caused more problems than if he were to leave now.

The amputation caused no pain. Their live schedule continued unabated though the band still refused to leave their native territory for the lights of the Big City, an unusual course to take, but a wise one as well. With two major record companies actively pursuing them (CBS had recently joined in the chase), Simple Minds had no need to try and prove themselves on the London circuit. They had established a firm local base and were capable of selling out 600 seater venues. It would have been stupid to move south and start everything again from scratch.

By remaining on their home territory Simple Minds also hoped to avoid the full glare of the media which would have been quite happy to give Simple Minds the 'big build up' if only the group would move to a more accessible area – meaning London. But the 'big build up' was the last thing Simple Minds wanted. Many are the bands who, early in their careers, have fallen foul of their admirers' good intentions, and Simple Minds had no intention of joining the casualty list. When, for instance, _Rolling Stone_ writer Jon Landau announced that he had seen the future of rock 'n' roll, ". . . and its name is Bruce Springsteen", neither he nor Springsteen could possibly have foreseen the phrase being taken up by journalists and ad-men the world over. And while there were enough people in the USA who had already seen Springsteen, and therefore had at least some conception of what Landau was talking about, the rest of the world remained either ignorant or cynical.

When Springsteen arrived in London in mid-1975 excitement was at fever pitch. The man's face was everywhere, staring out from magazines, bill hoardings, record shop windows. Tickets for Springsteen's Hammersmith shows were like gold dust. "Is London ready for Bruce Springsteen?", asked the record company

advertisements. Unfortunately, it was. When the future of rock 'n' roll turned out to be a skinny guy in a white T-shirt who sang songs about cars and girls and girls and cars, the backlash was as immediate as it was inevitable. Nobody could have expected anything less. The punters had been led to expect miracles. The second coming wouldn't have satisfied them.

By January 1979 Simple Minds had still to play their Hammersmith shows. But the warning signs were already there, as a second _New Musical Express_ review pointed out in that same month. "The many people who have stumbled across Simple Minds in Scotland know how wonderful they are. (But) don't blame the band for the enthusiasm of the media."

For that is what would happen. Just as Springsteen found out when he made his first trip to England, a major media build-up can quickly lead to a massive public turn off, especially when the band is not readily available for people to go out and see. For all the barriers broken down by the punk rock explosion, it was still expected for a band to have "paid its dues" before breaking into the big time. And to pay your dues, you had to be in London, your name haunting the gig guides as you moved slowly from the King's Head to the Marquee, the Marquee to the Music Machine, the Music Machine to the Hammersmith Odeon. To appear from nowhere and claim you were "really big in Scotland" just wasn't enough. In refusing to put themselves into the limelight, Simple Minds were not only distancing themselves from the full attention of the media, they were also divorcing themselves from the people who really mattered – the public.

"A lot of people think we've had it really easy because they didn't see us at the Hope and Anchor," said Jim. "And to be honest, we would rather have gone out and got a grass roots following. But we also wanted to get things straight. We wanted a proper studio, a proper sound, a proper producer. And obviously we couldn't have done that on our own."

Indeed they couldn't. But the alternative was to allow themselves to be pushed into a position whereby the band was literally forced into people's faces. Even Bruce Findlay was unable to resist Arista flexing its corporate muscle. Simple Minds, it was said, was going to

make the biggest splash ever.

On March 27 the band was unveiled on the *Old Grey Whistle Test*. For so long a stodgy joke, the programme had finally come to terms with the fact that there was life outside of the 20,000 seater halls, that there was more to rock than Rick Wakeman's latest "Henry VIII On Ice" extravaganza. With new presenter Anne Nightingale taking over from Bob Harris, *Whistle Test's* producer Mike Appleton gave the entire programme a face lift. Starting with Ms. Nightingale's first show, *Whistle Test* would now feature new bands fresh from the street. And Simple Minds, whose second demo tape had arrived just as Appleton was plotting his new schedule, was exactly the sort of group he was seeking.

Whistle Test would introduce the band to the country. A full British tour, opening for Magazine, would do the rest. Booking Simple Minds on to the tour had been an inspired move, to say the least. On the one hand you had the headliner, last year's critical darlings, now reeling from the total savaging of their second LP; and on the other, you had Simple Minds . . . this year's darlings.

The band's début album, "Life In A Day", was released midway through the tour in April 1979. It was symbolic that while it crashed straight into the chart before the tour had even reached London, Magazine was still waiting for their "Secondhand Daylight" LP to make the Top 30 long after the dates were finished. But perhaps the most telling moment of all came at the London gig itself when Simple Minds ran through a particularly spirited set at the Theatre Royal in Drury Lane.

They were halfway through their performance when, without warning, the entire sound system cut out. The band waited, horror-stricken, while their road crew frantically dashed around looking for the source of the problem. Somebody, it seemed, had pulled the plugs out on the band. All the plugs. And while nobody ever voiced their suspicions in public, the finger of doubt did point rather strongly in the direction of Magazine's own road crew. By the time power had been restored Simple Minds had lost all their momentum. They limped through the rest of the set, played a very perfunctory encore and looked like they wanted nothing more than to take an early bath, then go home to bed.

Yet when the evening's accolades were handed out, it was Simple Minds who came away not only with honours, but with an agency deal and a music publishing contract too. The band was hot.

"Life In A Day" was recorded initially at the Farmhouse Studios in Little Chalfont and the sessions eventually moved to the more illustrious Abbey Road studios in London.

It was at the Farmhouse Studios where Tony Stewart, from the *New Musical Express*, first caught up with Simple Minds. The ensuing encounter was spread over two sides of the magazine and Stewart took a very firm stand behind a band whom he saw as ". . . redefining the new sound of the Seventies which gives so much hope for rock 'n' roll in the Eighties. Simple Minds are one of the few (bands) to draw on the strings of the early to mid-Seventies and construct an accessible and commercial formula."

The inference was clear. Bands like XTC,

Magazine and The Only Ones, who shared similar musical roots with Simple Minds, were condemned almost by definition to forever stalk the lower reaches of the chart. Simple Minds was being groomed to step out of those shadows and take their music to a larger audience than their contemporaries could even dream of reaching.

Stewart's words, over the next few months, were to become almost a touchstone for Arista Records. When, as Jim Kerr remarked to Stewart, several of the major record companies had spent a large part of 1978 nursing badly burned fingers, Arista had been one of the severest casualties of all.

The year had begun with a popular upsurge in the fortunes of the "pop group". As Charlie Burchill had already observed, much of the excitement had gone out of punk rock. There was only a limited number of things you could say with three chords, a buzzsaw guitar and a vocabulary that revolved around being permanently fed up. So when Glen Matlock put together The Rich Kids, a high energy band who translated the previous year's nihilistic energies into a pure pop sensibility, the nation's tastemakers deemed that as the Sex Pistols had started last year's big thing, it was only fitting that an ex-Pistol should lead this year's one.

EMI had already signed up The Rich Kids. But in A&R offices throughout London record company executives who only twelve months before had thought "Anarchy" was the girl who unlocked the office door each morning were poised to descend on every able bodied pop group they could find.

And they found a lot. One by one fresh-faced young men who liked nothing more than to sit around and trade old Monkees' riffs with friends were being ushered wide eyed and wondering into recording studios. There, they were informed, they would make music that would shake the earth. Harvest had The Banned, RAK had The Autographs, UA had The Boyfriends, and Arista had The Pleasers. But none of them had the hits.

For whatever reason Power Pop just did not take off. It wasn't even taken seriously. Even the music press, who had started the whole thing off in the first place, didn't like it. The bands simply floundered against a wall of total apathy.

And one by one they faded away, leaving nothing behind beyond an irregular brown stain in the rock history books and a couple of indifferent singles to show their grandchildren.

It was into that climate that Simple Minds had first wandered. Then, nobody wanted to know them. Now everybody was pressing for their favours. And Arista were pressing harder than anybody. The Pleasers had bombed as ignominiously as any Power Popper, and the lessons, not to mention the expense, of that abortive campaign were still etched indelibly into the office walls. That was why Arista was so desperate for Simple Minds to succeed. Because nothing short of success would ever wipe away the memory of The Pleasers.

The man placed in charge of the sessions was producer John Leckie. It had been the band who first suggested using him. Leckie had produced "Real Life", the first album by Magazine, and a firm favourite with Simple Minds. He had also worked with two of the most important bands of the mid-Seventies – Be Bop Deluxe, for whom he co-produced two LPs, and the Doctors of Madness, whose second album Leckie alone masterminded. Since then, he had also sat at the controls for The Adverts, XTC and Advertising. When Bob Edmonds came up to Glasgow to discuss the sessions with Simple Minds, Leckie was unanimously voted the man they wanted. He was duly contacted and in January he journeyed up to Dundee to see the band in action at a University Freshers Ball. He was captivated within moments.

With "Life In A Day" Arista must have thought their every prayer had been answered. Even when the bad reviews began turning up, the general feeling was one of optimism. So what if Chris Bohn, in *Melody Maker*, described Simple Minds as ". . . a group of musical magpies who don't know what to do with all the ideas they've stolen". Far better to dwell on Tony Stewart's excited assertion that "Life In A Day" redefined the essence of rock and roll.

In actuality, the record fitted neither description. True, the album's influences did weigh heavily on the listener at times, but never so much as to obscure the value of the rest of the music. And while the moments of innovation were indeed sparkling, they merely lay down the foundations for what could one day see a revolution take place in the rock market-place.

The songs had all been composed by Jim and Charlie, with Jim taking an extra credit for the lyrics. And it was the lyrics which, on first hearing, most impressed. Not for their meaning – in most instances they were simply impressionistic fragments, strings of words laced together in such a way that any narrative powers they might have once had now gave way to a series of highly evocative word pictures. When he settled down to the task, as on "Chelsea Girl", Jim was quite capable of producing some very sharp, pithy observations.

The set opened with "Someone", a song which the band had featured on their second demo tape in December. An inspired choice for introducing the group to new listeners, "Someone" was a perfect marriage between Simple Minds' ability to play conventional rock and the more extreme tendencies with which they felt most comfortable. Jim's singing was self assured, a quirky echo of the seminal American outfit Sparks. The keyboards, too, hearkened back to the Mael brothers' finest moments, but if the delivery was somewhat derivative, the formula was away in a world of its own. "Someone" was a brisk and mature song, challenging enough to please the people lured into earshot by the band's reviews, but sufficiently accessible to satisfy the demands of a larger, less discerning audience.

Accessibility and challenge were the key elements of the entire album. There were enough reference points with which most people could identify yet "Life In A Day" was an almost startlingly original work. It was forever worrying at the boundaries of commercialism without once overstepping the mark. Gauche as they were, Simple Minds possessed an instinctive arrogance, an almost inbred belief in themselves which overwhelmed all other considerations. David Sinclair remembers their earliest live performances as being a prime example of this.

"Most young bands, when they first start out, think that they are the best thing in the world. They usually get it knocked out of them after three or four piss-awful pub gigs, but Simple Minds never did. They used to turn up at places like the Paisley Bungalow, which is not the most extravagant of settings, and they would have this massive light show, like they thought

they were Genesis! And whereas with any other band, everybody would just look at them and think, 'What prats! Who do they think they are?', Simple Minds could get away with it, simply because they did have this belief in themselves."

"Life In A Day", the album's title track and Simple Minds' first single, was the most

cavorting noisily around the microphones. John Leckie recorded the resultant sounds and treated them. Then, during the final mix, he suggested they be added to the synth break in "All For You". Thus originated the bizarre hisses which have so baffled present day music students!

Side one closed with "Pleasantly Disturbed", an eight-minute colossus which was the first song Jim and Charlie had written for Simple Minds. The overall impression was of the Velvet Underground, as they would have been had John Cale not been forced out by Lou Reed's urge to write some pop songs. That feeling was heightened by Charlie Burchill's chilling violin, the sound weaving in and out of the other instruments, pulling the song on towards its painful climax.

More than any other track on the album, the broodingly repetitive "Pleasantly Disturbed" reflected the sleeve notes' description of having been "recorded at a low temperature". It was cold and despairing; Jim's vocals were almost inhuman in their lack of emotion, a mood accentuated by their being largely unintelligible. As Tony Stewart remarked in his album review: "The lyrics could all be indecipherable but the songs would still make sense." With "Pleasantly Disturbed", you know that something nasty was going on, even if you weren't quite sure what it was.

"No Cure", which opened side two was a contrasting return to the lightweight Sparks vibe of "Someone", while the next song in the cycle, "Chelsea Girl", was a neon lit palace compared to the gloomy cathedrals erected by various other tracks. The title was borrowed from Nico, the closing refrain gave a passing nod to Roxy Music, and Be Bop Deluxe were somewhere in there as well. But the whole was much, much greater than the parts. When Arista chose this song as Simple Minds' second single not even the most impartial observer could have failed to be surprised when "Chelsea Girl" failed to emulate even its predecessor's lowly chart placing.

Lyrically the song was the most conventional on the album, attacking a girlfriend's rampant promiscuity with a resentment that cunningly masked genuine affection. But it was musically that the song really came into its own. Charlie Burchill's crashing power chords kept things on an even

recent song on the set. Above a sombre wall of sound, courtesy of McNeil's clinically precise keyboards, Jim Kerr's vocals hung detached and aloof. The song had few precedents, least of all the ". . . echoes of Magazine's 'Shot By Both Sides'," which *Sounds'* reviewer cited as one good reason for Jim to start watching out ". . . for those tell-tale signs of receding hair."

Next up were "Sad Affair" and "All For You", the former an abrupt and insistent slice of synthesizer-heavy moodiness, the latter a jaunty effort which dated back to Simple Minds' earliest demos. The song had, in fact, come close to being excluded from the album; it had been dropped from the live show almost eight months before, and was only revived when the band found themselves one song short during the sessions. It also featured the vinyl début of Bruce Findlay. Arriving at the studio drunk one evening, Bruce donned a pair of headphones and began

keel while all around the rest of the band pulled out all the stops. The most successful track on the album, "Chelsea Girl" didn't so much tread the tightrope between accessibility and obscurity as gleefully and fearlessly run along it. And disc jockeys like Anne Nightingale were quick to applaud Simple Minds' achievement, even if the public remained stubbornly unimpressed.

With any other band the rest of the album could have been an anticlimax after a song like "Chelsea Girl". And Simple Minds did seem to falter slightly with "Wasteland" and "Destiny", songs which returned to the fringes of rock 'n' roll, even if the mood was closer to Devo than The Dead. But Simple Minds still had one more trick up their sleeves.

"Murder Mystery" was another epic. If "Pleasantly Disturbed" had peered into the abyss, "Murder Mystery" held its breath and jumped right in. The vital ingredients – crooning violin, piping organ – were still there, ensuring that the spectre of The Velvets remained close at hand. But Simple Minds skilfully negotiated the pitfalls and crevices which might so easily have consumed them. With tongues placed very firmly in their cheeks, they carried the song along a path strewn with the corpses of bands incapable of avoiding the traps. The song's shuddering climax paid tribute to the greatest band of them all, The Doctors of Madness, the only other group to have flirted as successfully with The Velvet's *femme fatale* appeal.

So the acknowledged influences were manifest, the imposed ones equally so. But that could in no way detract from the potency of Simple Minds' brew. Accused of peppering the album with "obsessive monochromatic scenarios", Jim was to retaliate: "People say we're deliberately weird. But we're not trying to be, although we're no Joe Ordinaries either. It would be easy to be weird for the sake of it, but that is the easy way out. We try hard to put soul and feeling into every song that we do. Passion is important to move people. And there is a lot of humour in our songs.

"They have looked at us, and groups like us, and said 'art school rock'. Art school rock! We're fucking closer to bricklayers and plumbers. It's just stupid. They say we're Moderne lads with silly eye mascara, making pointless, cold music, all alienated and everything. I should

fucking well think we feel alienated, coming from the Gorbals where, if you weren't totally into football and girls, there was something really the matter with you, and where it was really difficult for you to do anything like music. I wish there was a decent title, much as I don't like them, for bands like Roxy, Magazine and us. Like when you get two R 'n' B bands, you don't compare the sound, you look at them both and that's R 'n' B. There should be a reasonable title to use.

"This kind of music takes your mind further out. It's trying to take steps ahead in rock music generally, into unknown areas. For example, when listening to Eno, you suddenly realise he's taking steps out there. Compare it to the desert. Nothing happens out there, no-one wants to go out there, and it's the same with music. There are areas where no-one will go near, they feel it's too unappealing or too unusual. They feel uncomfortable. This type of music moves out there."

3

"JESUS, WHERE'S THE 'CHELSEA GIRL'?"

"When it was first recorded, the band really liked the album," Brian Hogg declared. "But as time went by they became less and less happy about it. They had tried to change the songs around a bit and really it didn't work. A lot of the songs had been written while there were still two guitarists in the band. After Duncan Barnwell left, and particularly on the album, they tried to compensate by moving Mick McNeil's keyboards further forward. But nobody had any real idea how the keyboards should be used. They weren't particularly subtle on that album."

Another factor in the band's disillusionment with the record, which Jim and Charlie were both to acknowledge, was their unfamiliarity with recording studios. On first hearing yourself booming out of studio speakers the sound is incredibly powerful, but those noises bear very little resemblance to what will eventually appear on vinyl. As Charlie Burchill so succinctly put it. "You hear the record for the first time and you just think 'What the fuck is *that*?' "

But, as Brian Hogg claims, the biggest problem with the album was totally out of the band's hands. "Bruce and I were really upset when the band started badmouthing the album, mainly because we felt they were doing it in retrospect. The album really got mangled by the press, Simple Minds felt they had to redeem their reputation. The easiest way of doing that was to disassociate themselves from the album."

For the next year Simple Minds' interviews were to be peppered with barbs directed solely at "Life In A Day". Everything from the way it had been recorded to the way it was promoted seemed to incur their wrath, as Jim was to later explain. "It was so ham-fisted, bandied about. The LP came in at number 32, the single was like 68, and Arista had these big ads saying 'hit single, hit album'. We got that high in the chart with comparatively low sales, (simply) because nothing else was happening in the music scene." In a month when the top three singles came from Art Garfunkel, Boney M and the Village People, it was not difficult to discern his meaning.

Simple Minds were also beginning to feel the first effects of the massive build-up they had been given. When people came to see them live,

it was not because they had liked the records or enjoyed checking out new acts. It was because, "I heard you sounded like David Bowie/Magazine/Ultravox (delete as applicable), so I thought I'd come along."

In the pages of the music press, too, the backlash was beginning to make itself felt. With the band cocooned in the relative safety of Glasgow, only the most hardened London-based writers would make the long trek up to see them. The rest of the group's press came from local writers, most of whom were personal friends of the band anyway. But now Simple Minds were on display for anybody to see. As soon as the Magazine tour ended the band embarked on their own series of dates around the country. And for those writers who had been left out in the cold while their more enlightened colleagues waxed lyrical about this latest Scottish export, the opportunity to make their own

feelings heard was too great to be resisted.

The first hints of a change in the weather came with the album's reception in the weekly review columns. Aside from Tony Stewart's glowing character reference, "Life In A Day" was viewed with the utmost suspicion by those staff writers entrusted with giving the record a fair and honest hearing. Few of them could see what all the fuss had been about.

Says Brian Hogg: "The band really did suffer when the album came out. It was as if nobody could stomach the fact that they had come up from nowhere, without any help from the establishment – the small clubs, the papers, people like that. There was an incredible amount of resentment flying around. Like one week Howard Thompson from CBS was guest singles' reviewer in *Sounds*. And it just happened to be the week 'Chelsea Girl' came out. Now, CBS had been really keen on signing Simple Minds, they would have moved Heaven and hell to get them. But the band came to us, so when Howard found 'Chelsea Girl' sitting in the pile of singles he was to review, he really went to town on it. It was things like that, they really upset the band.

"People were shouting 'hype' as well, which was pissing us off. The band had been so adamant when they signed that there was to be no hype. There would be none of these limited edition picture discs going out to the chart return shops, none of that. The group wanted to be taken on their own merits, not on a string of gimmicks. But once again, because they had just come out of nowhere, everybody's back immediately went up. I think the band were complaining about everything simply as a reaction to what they were going through."

Simple Minds spent much of the spring and summer touring and immediately found themselves up against some startling home truths. Despite the chart success of the records, despite the packed houses calling them back for encores every night on the Magazine tour, their own tour of the clubs around the country was very sparsely attended. And to make matters worse they were all but unable to play the one town where they would have drawn a capacity crowd: Glasgow.

"We're really restricted in Glasgow," Charlie told *Sounds*. "There isn't anywhere for us to play because of size, organisation and that kind of thing. We played a college gig a while back, it was a tiny little hall and there were five hundred people in it and no bouncers anywhere.

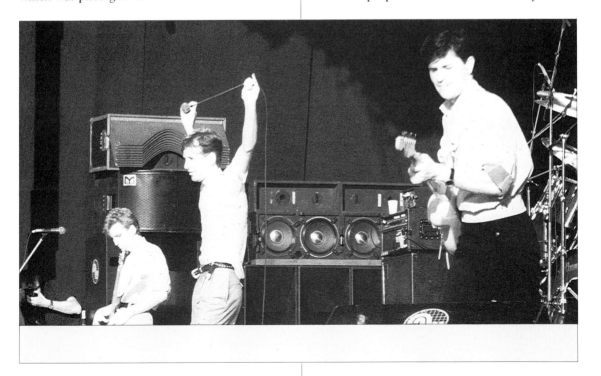

projecting yourself above them, ultimately for them to enjoy it. People think it's an arrogant pose but it isn't really."

Anxious to make amends after what they considered a disastrous début, Simple Minds returned to the recording studios in late summer with John Leckie again in tow. The fruits of the sessions were delivered to Arista as one complete package: "Real To Real Cacophony".

In an interview with *ZigZag* Jim said: "We told Arista we'd got all these great songs and they said OK, do them. When we played them the album they said 'What's this?' So we showed them the cover, just plain blue, and they said 'It's horrible!' " Arista, Jim related, hated what they heard. "They went 'Jesus, where's the "Chelsea Girl"?', and we said 'Well, there isn't one . . .' "

During the interviews which surrounded the release of "Life In A Day", Simple Minds

It was bedlam." Jim Kerr echoed these remarks: "I don't really enjoy playing Glasgow," he said. "It's a weird place for a band at our stage. When you first start off everyone in Glasgow gets right behind you. But there isn't much going on in Glasgow, so when you get a band that's getting on a bit, everybody really gets jealous. It's like 'those up there, those cunts. It could've been me.' "

Despite their youth Simple Minds had already honed performing live down to a fine art. In the early days they had experimented heavily with lighting effects and stage make-up. As their career gained momentum the band began to place less reliance on such blatant visuals, but they retained the spirit that had encouraged them to use them in the first place. "When we begin a show it's a menacing thing," Jim stated. "It's intimidating, as if we're taking a stand against the audience. It's a case of

had promised that their next album would be totally different. "We're going to experiment to try and get a sound of our own," Jim told *Sounds*. "The next LP will be much more us. I don't think it'll be so much of the 'Simple Minds sound like this or that'. Some of that we could take, but some of it really got on our nerves. Especially XTC and things like that. People always look to compare a new band with someone else."

The recording of "Real To Real Cacophony", at Rockfield Studios in Monmouth, was veiled in secrecy. Reporters were barred from the premises. Even Arista had little idea of what Simple Minds were up to.

"They felt that too many people in the business had heard the demos for 'Life In A Day'," explained Brian Hogg. "So for the new album they kept everything under wraps. They didn't play any of the new songs live, they just

wrote the whole thing in the studio. Which is why 'Real To Real Cacophony' sounds so claustrophobic. It was conceived entirely in the studio, I don't think the band even thought about how the songs would come over in concert. It's like the ultimate studio album, and it works really well."

Jim later elaborated: "We didn't demo anything before we went in. All we had were cassettes with little bits on. We just went in and did it, and that's going to be our attitude from now on. On edge, where you have to make spot decisions. It wasn't safe and that felt good.

"We knew we had to get a sound of our own. We talked with John Leckie about what we wanted, and we questioned everything, even in the vocals. On the first album they were so held back, bland and smooth. But this time I just wrote everything down, sat back for half an hour and worked it all out, then I'd go in and say, 'Right, let's do it', and catch the spontaneous feel. That's where it all comes from."

Reviewing "Real To Real Cacophony", *Sounds* described the record as "probably the most uncommercial album ever released by Arista U.K." It was an accurate observation. Even taking into account some of the totally unsaleable vinyl turkeys for which the company had been responsible, "Real To Real Cacophony" was so densely uncompromising that "Life In A Day" sounded positively vibrant when placed against it. From being a mirror of other people's musical preoccupations, Simple Minds was now a plate of black steel, absorbing light and life and converting it into base negativism. When Jim Kerr spoke of Eno taking steps out in the desert, you knew that the balding dilettante was no longer alone out there.

"There was always an ambition to be in a progressive band, not to just get up and boogie, or whatever," Jim told *ZigZag*. "People look at our ambition and see that we're trying to do something a bit different, in new ways, and they think we're trying to do something above the rest, kind of detached, like we're not one of the boys. But in order for music to progress you must take steps forward."

Charlie continued: "Speaking musically, I think everything that is going to be done has been done within the confines of musical notes. So what I feel you have to do is sort of stretch people's imagination, to open up. It's like escapism, really."

"We do have a passion to be one step ahead," Jim added. "Not so as to look back and say 'Oh, we were ahead then'. It's just a natural thing within us that we are interested in doing something new."

The album's key was alienation. In "Calling Your Name", Jim sang of the frustration of trying to get out of Glasgow, while "Veldt" was swamped in the sounds of the jungle, conjuring up pictures of darkness and primitivism. There was a tune, barely, but it wasn't one you'd want to whistle. "There were a lot of secret facts about what was happening in Cambodia coming out on the news, that really inspired us," Jim explained in that same *ZigZag* interview. "But how can you accept the news? I suppose we could have put words to 'Veldt', telling everyone how bad it was, but . . ."

The lightest and – by popular opinion – weakest moment on the set came with "Changeling". This was the track selected by Arista for the band's third single, an action which highlighted a strange contradiction in the band's attitude. They were fiercely stubborn, steadfastly resisting the record company's suggestions that they continue to mine the vein opened by "Life In A Day". But they were quite happy to give Arista a free hand when it came to selecting singles. "We just listen to the promotion department, or whoever it is that will take the song to the BBC," Jim explained. "They should know best what stands the best chance."

The best chance of what? It seemed strange for a band to be concerned with hit records when they had just spent two months creating an album that was the very antithesis of conventional 'hit formulae'.

If the faintly Numan-esque "Changeling" was the only track on the album that could remotely be considered single material, Arista's complaints about the record's paucity of selling points were justified. And just to emphasise its total lack of faith in the LP, the record company quietly slipped both single and album into their December release schedules, obviously hoping that both would get lost in the pre-Christmas rush for Pink Floyd's "The Wall". Maybe such an abject failure would force Simple Minds to see the error of their ways.

The tour which had been set up to promote the album was actually finished by the time "Real To Real Cacophony" reached the record shops. Simple Minds were left with nothing to occupy their minds while, all around, their efforts were regarded with lame indifference. But far from despairing, the band was able to regard this latest creation with a great deal of satisfaction.

"I'd love to hear what the reaction would have been if the album had been our first," Jim mused. "Because in some ways it is our first. We had an attitude of our own, we had more of a hand in the production. We felt we could incorporate each instrument better."

To back up that last remark, he needed only to point to Charlie Burchill's surprisingly proficient sax playing; surprising because the guitarist had only bought the instrument a week

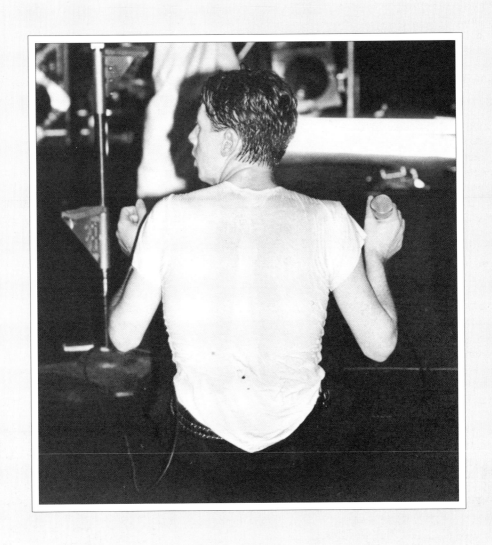

before. The first time he ever tried playing it was on the album! "I think it's great to mix competence with incompetence," Jim announced.

Appearances on the *Old Grey Whistle Test* and the John Peel show bracketed the album's release, their performances collected and dignified. Simple Minds had come a long way from the days when, as an inexperienced group of unknowns, they had arrived at one radio session uncertain of even how to tune their instruments. On the road they had grown in stature too: during their first headlining tour of England Jim had repeatedly rushed offstage in mid-set to throw up, but nerves and insecurity were now a thing of the past. Yet, Simple Minds had very little reason for feeling so confident.

Relations with Arista were becoming very shaky. Internal record company politics had seen a whole new régime move in to the Cavendish Square offices. People who had been around when Simple Minds first signed were on their way out, and with them went the friendship and belief in what the group were doing. The new staff had very little time or patience for Simple Minds. "Real To Real Cacophony" might have been a very impressive album from an artistic

point of view, but Arista was not in business to make artistic statements. The label wanted to sell records, lots of them, and Simple Minds were very obviously not doing that.

The fate of Zoom Records was also hanging on a thread. Simple Minds apart, the Edinburgh label had yet to produce any artist capable of attracting attention. And Simple Minds, because of their initial financial demands, weren't even a Zoom band according to the contracts.

Matters came to a head just as the first year of Zoom's distribution deal ended. Bruce Findlay arrived at the Arista offices bearing a tape of Zoom's projected new single by Tony Pilley – better known as the owner of the Barclay Towers studio. Arista refused point blank to have anything to do with it. Bruce indignantly pointed to the contract stipulation that stated Arista was responsible only for distributing and marketing Zoom product. Arista pulled out the magnifying glass and indicated the small print which demanded every release had to match up to certain technical and commercial standards. Quite what these standards were the contract did not say. But the Tony Pilley single did not reach them. Bruce offered to re-record

the single. Arista promised to turn that down as well. It was a hopeless situation, and Bruce knew it. But, as he discovered when he tried to negotiate a new deal for Zoom with another record company, few people had any patience with a small independent whose only saleable act was already signed, in a separate deal, to somebody else. In February 1980, Zoom Records folded for good.

But Bruce had not escaped from Arista yet. Simple Minds still had another year of their contract left to run, and despite the corporate hatred of "Real To Real Cacophony", Arista had no intention of allowing the band out of their grasp. Simple Minds still commanded some respect in music business circles, if only for their staunch refusal to obey the commercial norm. They had credibility, and that was very important to a record company whose biggest selling artist was Barry Manilow, and whose only other influential rock artists – Lou Reed, Patti Smith, and Iggy Pop – were either negotiating new contracts elsewhere, retiring from the music business, or burning out very slowly and painfully.

There was always the chance, however slim, that having got "Real To Real Cacophony"

out of their systems, Simple Minds would now return to the formulae which had so attracted Arista in the first place. *New Musical Express'* Glenn Gibson might have described "Real To Real Cacophony" as being "far more commercial than others would have you believe", but Arista was certain that, with a little bit more pressure, Simple Minds could do a lot better than that.

Pressure. The band which had started life as a simple hobby were now up to their necks in the machinations of Big Business. They had responsibilities now, and albums like "Real to Real Cacophony" were a luxury that Simple Minds just could not afford. They were heavily in debt; were the band to offer themselves to other record companies they would find very few willing to gamble on such a poor financial risk.

It was with that threat hanging over their head that Simple Minds re-entered Rockfield studios, with John Leckie still at the helm, to begin work on their third album.

4

WE TRAVEL

In the autumn of 1979 Simple Minds set off on their first tour of Europe and America. The American trip was short, highlighted only by a well-received appearance at one of New York's premier niteries, Hurrahs. Europe, again given only a fleeting glimpse of the band, was a little more promising, and in the new year Simple Minds returned for a more extensive visit.

This tour lasted six weeks, and it was during the trip that the band's ideas for the third album begin to coalesce. Even from the back of a car, Europe was a continual barrage of inspiration. Observations would be jotted down in notebooks, observations which brought home to the band just how isolated they were living on an island. Events in one country, which can cause major repercussions throughout the European mainland, reach Britain as ripples, occasionally disrupting but never really disturbing the fabric of life. With this realisation, the band saw their aims very clearly. If they were to make an album that fully embraced their European experiences, as they intended to do, it would have to embrace the ugliness as well as the beauty, the refugees as well as the monarchies.

It was all too easy for bands to sing of 'Europa' in those days. It was as if the mere mention of the continent could bring life to the direst of monologues. When, to quote one of Jim Kerr's favourite examples, The Automatics sang "When The Tanks Are Rolling Over Poland", nobody knew what they were on about, but it sounded good anyway. All you had to do was throw in an Austrian city name, and a wealth of meaninglessness suddenly became deeply profound. It meant nothing to anyone, but the idea of "New Europeans" wandering around with their headphones on was a very evocative one all the same.

What Simple Minds wanted to do was incorporate experience into their music. As they were to say on many occasions, they had spent much of 1980 touring Europe, meeting people, talking to people. In a way, singing about Europe was a far more honest thing for Simple Minds to do than if they came out with an album of songs about being on the dole in Glasgow.

"We do run a giant risk of getting labelled as pretentious, being Glasgow boys and singing about Europe," said Kerr. "But you can't blind yourself and pretend that nothing exists outside your home town. We're not trying to solve the problems of the world or anything like that, but we are showing that we don't just sit in the recording studio and assume that there's nothing happening in the outside world."

There was, in fact, a lot happening, and as the album began to take shape, Simple Minds saw themselves creating a record which was not so much a series of holiday snapshots as a musical documentary as valid as any BBC newsreel. The assassination of Ulrike Meinhof, the massive military manoeuvres to which the band were witness as they drove between Düsseldorf and Berlin, the constant air of East-West confrontation that permeates Berlin. All of this was absorbed, then spewed out into the songs. The album would deal in contrasts, pitching the romantic images of Europe so cherished by the band's contemporaries against the harsh realities of living with one super power on your doorstep and another one in your potting shed.

"The idea of a Moscow dominated world really freaks me out," Jim confided in an interview with *Record Mirror*. "But a Los Angeles dominated world frightens me every bit as much. Maybe I should be writing about life in the disco or something, but then I pick up the paper and read that every house in Switzerland has an in-built fucking fall-out shelter! You can't ignore things like that!

"With lyrics, sometimes you say something and you think it's really yukky and pretentious. There's words like 'war' – I'd never used them, they're so strong. But when you go and see things it's even more pretentious to think everything is safe."

Just as "Real To Real Cacophony" had seen the band shift direction very sharply away from "Life In A Day", so they approached their third album from a totally fresh angle. Whereas the first two albums had been based on drama, peaking and receding, the new set would deal with repetition. They aimed for a dance-orientated sound, an album that would sound as good on the front room stereo as on the biggest disco sound-system. Jim related to *Record Mirror* how during the February tours, the band went into a club in Berlin and heard "Premonition" slipping effortlessly in alongside Donna Summer, Talking Heads and Ohio Players. The experience

brought home to them just how much their attitudes had changed. In the old days, the band would have been content merely to have people come along to see them and enjoy themselves. But now, the biggest thrill was to make people dance, seeing them moving unselfconsciously to the music, careless of what was going on around them. That, Jim assured *Record Mirror*, was "a real brilliant buzz. You know disco being 'Y.M.C.A.' and all that stuff. It would be great for us to hear something like 'I Travel' (the new single) in a disco."

"I Travel", a convoluted dance song, linked together a series of connected statements, building up to what was almost a travelogue. The hit and run assassins and the airports playing "Bi Some Lio"; the images all came together in a frenzied rush, while underneath a furious backing propelled the song irresistibly along. "I think if we can do a song that's

appealing, but with an edge so it doesn't get too comfortable, people might listen to what's being said," Jim commented on "I Travel".

The track opened "Empires And Dance", Simple Minds' third album. Lyrically it complemented the twin themes of power and decay on the LP sleeve. A chipped military statue, a timeless leader, stood grim-faced against a backdrop of modern Athens; cities, buildings, falling down. The ruins of the Parthenon were set in harsh relief against the twilight sky.

It was, on the surface, merely a fresh reworking of the same old ideas; elegance and decadence set against a throbbing back beat. But Simple Minds delved under the skin of their subject, probing and prodding into places few other bands had ventured. When Jim sang of the marching men of Central Europe, the image was not the usual one of war, but of a situation which, in insular Great Britain, was

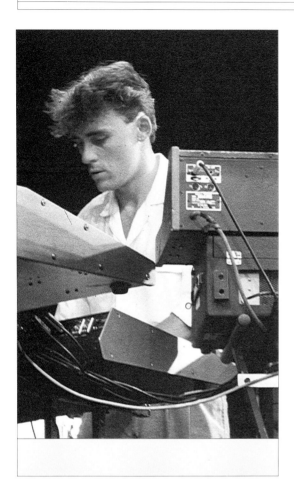

unimaginable. As Jim remarked to the *New Musical Express*: "Even when you see Northern Ireland on the television you might get a bit concerned, but you tend to dismiss it as just something on the TV tube.

"We were driving through East Germany (and) it was like going from a colour picture into black and white, no neon lights for sixty miles. Just before you go into the Western sector of Berlin, there are these Russian tanks, troops and missiles everywhere. Even through a van window, how can you not be affected by something like that?"

Yet Simple Minds had no intention of using the album as a political rostrum. Just as "Veldt" on "Real To Real Cacophony" had used images rather than words to convey its mood, so "Empires And Dance" remained firmly ambiguous, observing rather than judging. In an interview with *ZigZag*, Jim indicated this impartial stance by slamming those self-appointed spokesmen who treat the stage as a pulpit, preaching their own quick and easy panaceas to the masses.

"Once you get behind a microphone you have a degree of power and people look up to you. But then you get stuff that is really condescending, like telling how bad war is. I mean big deal! Everyone knows that.

"I think we are a bit vague in a way. I don't think we have ever put our head on a block and said 'This is fact!' because I don't think we know anything as 100% fact. I mean, political wise there are plenty of good themes for songs, but who really knows who is right?"

This confusion was confronted in "I Travel". Europe has a language problem, Jim sang. So does America, so does Asia. The language problem was politics, and it didn't matter where you went, how much you travelled,

the problem was always there. "At times I feel dead guilty mentioning anything political because I don't vote, and you know what a waste that is. But I'm not going to vote until I've done enough research on it". If people would only research, the song was saying, the problem would no longer be there.

If "I Travel" was extroverted, a celebration of the ability to move from place to place, the opposite end of the spectrum was approached in "Thirty Frames A Second", a song heavy with retrospection.

"The song was a lot heavier when I wrote it," Jim informed the *New Musical Express*. "It was about a man who becomes a father, but he no longer recognises his children because they haven't made the same mistakes that he did. They reject his food and everything. But it turns out to be the song of a man looking back, trying to grasp what purpose there is in existing."

The autobiographical mood of the song made "Thirty Frames A Second" an intensely personal experience, somewhat at odds with the impersonal, impartial moods conveyed by the record. But coming as it did towards the end of the album, followed only by two short, sombre instrumental pieces, "Thirty Frames A Second"

brought the listener back to a reality which was very different from that of the other songs. "Capital City", for instance, dealt with the outbreak of civil war, but the treatment was one of narration, as by a foreign newsman viewing the unrest from a safe room in his embassy. "This Fear Of Gods" was also an observation, rather than a participation. As its title implied, the song was concerned with religion, and the hold it has on people. The emotions which "This Fear Of Gods" aroused would not have been unfamiliar to much of Catholic Europe.

But all this talk of Europe and Europeans was not a concept that Simple Minds' continental following would have been able to grasp. Charlie admitted as much in an interview with *New Musical Express*.

"People (over here) start labelling things as 'European' and they have only a really vague idea of what they mean by it. In Germany or Holland, the whole musical idea of 'the Europeans' means nothing. It doesn't even exist! The only people to whom that whole thing exists are the readers of the British music papers." And it was on that premise that "Empires And Dance" won its greatest triumph. In steering clear of the musical élitism which made 'Europa' a separate entity, whose sole purpose was to donate picturesque images to nonsensical verses. Simple Minds created a unity out of the thousand diverse currents which they felt running through the continent, without falling into the traps of romanticism.

The image of Europe, so popularly misconceived by other talents, had been given a battering from which it would never recover. A year later Richard Strange was to build upon the shattered remains to create "The Phenomenal Rise Of Richard Strange", a political song cycle whose nightmare visions of a single European state could never have been conceived without at least some reference to "Empires And Dance".

Meanwhile, Simple Minds' ambitions were to come in for attack from a totally unexpected quarter. Jim frequently questioned the stereotyping which demanded all Scottish bands stick to the things they knew about. He

told *ZigZag*: "I had a kind of argument with Richard Jobson (of The Skids) who said we were betraying our heritage by playing all this funk, black and European music. We should be getting a young sound of Scotland going. I was saying that we just don't get any heather or stuff in Glasgow. We're from a different part of Scotland to The Skids. When I first met them I couldn't understand a word they were saying, their accents were so thick!"

Simple Minds had, in fact decided very early on that they did not want to be roped into any so-called Scottish scene, especially that breed espoused by The Skids. That band gleefully embraced their roots, po-faced as their music struggled to blend post-punk rock and roll with prehistoric Celtic music. Simple Minds, on the other hand, were emphatic in their disavowal of such musical patriotism. There would be no bagpipes on their records. Over the years they have broached the subject in many interviews, often having to defend their motives against the likes of both Richard Jobson and those journalists who like to have everything neatly pigeon-holed for future reference.

As Jim pointed out to *New Musical Express*: "People make too much of where a group comes from. (They) expect us to be very Scottish, very patriotic and proud of our roots . . . Because we come from Glasgow they expect us to be even more like that. But I think it alienates people if you play too much on it. If people start liking various groups just because they come from Sheffield or Liverpool, it gets like football. Music is about sound, isn't it? It's about heart. It's not about what's happening in the background or what's behind it. It's something that provokes a *reaction*."

Simple Minds' new records certainly provoked a reaction. Although it wasn't a hit, "I Travel" caused something of a stir in the dance clubs. "Empires And Dance" itself did get into the Top 50, albeit at a lowly number 41. And nobody was happier than Arista, even though they were now barely on speaking terms with Simple Minds. The success of "Empires And Dance" encouraged them to persevere with the band, even though their contract had only another six months to run.

For Simple Minds, those six months stretched ahead like an eternity. "We thought we'd just be dropped," Jim later remarked. "But when it came to the crunch . . . We'd just get some good reviews for 'Empires And Dance' and we were getting a bit of reaction in Europe so they weren't prepared to let us go as easily as we'd hoped. We were well sick!"

Other people, too, were not slow to applaud the band's new direction. Concerts began to attract larger and more enthusiastic audiences than in the past. Simple Minds' name once more started to attach itself to terms like 'potential' and 'bright future'. And the group found themselves attracting the attention of other musicians who, just a few years before, had been on the level of demi-gods to them. During the recording of "Empires and Dance" at Rockfield word filtered through to them that David Bowie was recording in the studio next door. Simple Minds immediately ran in to ask the great man to play sax on their own record. Bowie had, in fact, dropped by to look in on Iggy Pop, whose latest LP, "Soldier", was being painfully pieced together. The two had written a new song for the album, "Play It Safe", and when Simple Minds wandered up, Bowie immediately handed them lyric sheets and roped them in to sing backing vocals with him. It didn't

seem to matter when Bowie proved unable to repay the favour.

Not long after that Simple Minds were given another very pleasant surprise. Amongst the handful of influential admirers won by "Real To Real Cacophony" was Peter Gabriel. He was setting out on a European tour in the autumn; perhaps Simple Minds would like to be his guests?

Since relinquishing his post as frontman with Genesis, Gabriel had been responsible for three very diverse albums in his own right, all of which he called "Peter Gabriel". Like Simple Minds, he had acquired a reputation for contrariness, especially when it came to keeping his record company happy. Gabriel's latest album had been described by his American label as commercial suicide, repulsing them so much that they returned his contract almost as quickly as they returned his tapes! The album, incidentally, went on to become Gabriel's most successful to date. But by that time another company had already snatched it up.

Gabriel was also very popular on the continent, and his offer to pay Simple Minds' expenses throughout the tour came as a blessed windfall. The band was so far in debt by this

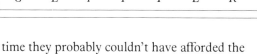
time they probably couldn't have afforded the fare to the airport, let alone financed a whole tour. And Gabriel's itinerary covered the entire continent, taking in both Simple Minds' own usual strongholds as well as ". . . exotic places like Portugal, Greece and Italy," where they had never been before.

For Jim the biggest thrill was the mere proximity of the benevolent Mr. Gabriel. "The first gig I ever saw was Genesis, when Gabriel was in the band. I really liked the presence of him especially. His approach to things was pretty intense; one minute he could be some monster, then the next, soft and gentle. The bit in between was unnerving because I couldn't decide whether he was a headbanger or totally sane. It was never far out hippy stuff, there was always a menace in what he did."

5

SONS AND SINNERS

Back in Britain, with European acclaim still loud in their ears, Simple Minds sat back to wait out the last few weeks of their Arista contract. It is hard to say which was the more disillusioned party; Simple Minds, whose fairy godfather had suddenly turned into a very wicked witch, or Arista, for whom the goose that had once promised to lay numerous golden eggs now looked suspiciously like a turkey, and a barren one at that. They had no interest in this bird's activities. When a new album was delivered Arista grudgingly pressed up 7,000 copies and then forgot about it. Then, a fortnight later, when orders for another 21,000 came in, they weren't able to meet the demand. And when the turkey finally announced it was going to fly the nest, Arista couldn't get it out of the door quick enough.

Or so it seemed from the outside. In reality the severance was both slow and painful. If Simple Minds hadn't been able to escape from the deal, Jim later said, they would have split up. As it was they had to surrender future royalties on all three albums to date simply to offset the debts they had incurred. But the band did not regret having fallen into such dire financial straits. Jim told the *New Musical Express*: "We're only in debt through trying to make things better for the group, getting out of the contract and making sure we've got the best possible equipment and the best instruments and everything. The only thing we've been guilty of is making a substandard first album."

"It's been two years since that LP," Charlie added. "But we're still being judged by it as a group. It's getting to be an albatross! I think Tony Stewart did a good review of it when it came out. He put it into perspective and said that we could do something worthwhile if we were given a decent chance."

Being out of the stifling atmosphere of Arista would, at long last, give Simple Minds the opportunity of proving Stewart right . . . or wrong. In a move which, at the time, seemed very much like jumping from frying pan to fire, Simple Minds had barely finished ripping up their old contract before they signed a new one. This time it was with Virgin Records, a company whose hippy-go-lucky image concealed a sabre toothed aggression that made Arista look positively benign.

"Now we have D.A.F. coming out of the offices instead of Barry Manilow," Jim quipped. But the reasons behind selecting Virgin were a lot more concrete than a simple matter of musical taste. In their short history Virgin had become one of the U.K.'s most successful record companies ever. Their roster consistently creamed off the very best of contemporary talent, and their sales record was second to none.

At the end of the 1960's Virgin boss Richard Branson was editing *Student* magazine and running a small mail order company which specialised in import albums. From there, it was but a small step to opening his own shop, and after that, a record company, Virgin Records.

The first release, in 1973, was "Tubular Bells", an album length instrumental piece by Mike Oldfield. It was an instant hit, elevating its 20-year-old composer to instant genius status, and his accountant to seventh heaven. The

record stayed in the chart for several years, calmly and assuredly outselling almost everything in sight. Even subsequent Oldfield albums had no chance of taming the monster "Bells". In 1976, Virgin estimated that "Tubular Bells" had found its way into five million homes worldwide. Eight years later there can be few people left in the Western world who haven't

have all been Virgin's at one time or another, and they didn't have to maintain any vows of chastity either.

But when Simple Minds pledged their troth to the label in March 1981, they were not simply throwing in their lot with a well-to-do record label. Among their label-mates were bands of the calibre of Magazine, XTC, PIL, The Human League and B.E.F. Their presence alone was proof enough that Virgin was capable of handling bands who weren't particularly renowned for their desire to turn out the chart toppers. The Human League, in fact, were on the verge of finally hitting it very big indeed. Their "Dare" album was in the last stages of completion, and the A&R department was preparing to milk it of every last potential hit single. By the end of 1981 Human League could look back on thirty-six weeks in the singles chart, a third of that spent in the top ten. It was into this rarefied atmosphere of success without compromise that Simple Minds plunged in March. Returning home from a short U.S. club tour, Virgin ushered them into the studio within days of their arrival, insistent that the band make a fresh start immediately.

They returned to Farmhouse studios, where "Life In A Day" had first taken shape. But instead of the faithful John Leckie, the man behind the control panel was another Virgin property, Steve Hillage. Charlie explained the reasons behind the move to *Sounds*: "We wanted a change from John Leckie purely because we wanted to see what the difference was. We heard this track by Ken Lockie (yet another Virgin artist) and it sounded amazing. We asked who produced it and they said it was Steve Hillage.

"And we thought: 'Old Cabbage Head!'," Jim laughingly added. "We'd never heard him before, but I knew Steve's image and there was a giant contrast with ours. But we met him and he was talking about a lot of European bands – Can and Neu! – and it just seemed we had that in common."

Steve Hillage was probably the last person anybody would have thought of associating with a group like Simple Minds. Indeed, the band did come in for a lot of criticism once word leaked out. Yet in his own fashion Hillage was as innovative as any of the trendier young producers whom outside observers felt

heard at least part of it.

After "Tubular Bells" neither Oldfield nor Branson needed ever to work again. But of course they did. Oldfield releases a new album every year or so, quietly unassuming little efforts which keep his name in the chart and his bank balance in the black. Branson sits behind his desk, peering over the paperwork at an empire that now encompasses virtually every avenue of mass communication open to the intrepid young businessman. He runs shops, owns a club, publishes books, makes films. He even flies a passenger airline. His record company, in any given week, can be found lurking somewhere around the Top Ten, and a flick through Virgin's back catalogue is like taking a crash course in the preoccupations of rock and pop for the last decade. Robert Wyatt, Gong, Anthony Moore, Can, Sparks, The Sex Pistols, Penetration, Culture Club, Genesis, The Flying Pickets; they

the band should be using. As a member of the legendary Gong in the mid-Seventies, it had been Hillage's musical knowledge which turned the band away from the chaotic wanderings for which they were renowned and into a coherent if somewhat unstable unit. Under his guidance Gong's penchant for the absurd was to spawn some of the era's most intriguing music, including a series of albums whose subject matter revolved around flying teapots, pot-head pixies, and Witch Yoni's pussy.

The band eventually disintegrated in 1975 and although various ex-members have kept the name and spirit alive ever since, it was the Hillage-inspired incarnation that is most fondly remembered. Hillage himself went on to record several solo albums, and his severance from his former partners indicated that he had lost none of his previous interest in the paranormal. In 1977, when even old colleagues like Daevid Allen were making concessions to contemporary punk fashion, Hillage was proudly informing visiting journalists that cabbages were an intelligent life form. His "L" solo album featured one track recorded purely during a full moon, and rumours quickly spread that throughout his stint with Simple Minds Hillage

kept a potted tree in the studio so he could have someone to talk to.

Eccentric, weird, or just plain batty, Steve Hillage's presence in the studio was a positive boon to Simple Minds. His quiet encouragement, his ability to inspire without apparently lifting a finger, saw the band produce their most consistent body of work to date. So relaxed were the proceedings that within a matter of weeks Simple Minds had completed fifteen backing tracks. This, Jim informed *Sounds*, made it imperative for them to think in terms of a double album. "Our songs never tend to be just 3½ minutes so we knew from the start there was too much. A lot of the tracks we do, because of the repetition, you *need* so much length before you can get inside it."

There has always been a deep seated prejudice against double albums. Ever since The Mothers of Invention introduced the idea to rock music in 1965, the very mention of a two LP set has conjured up awful visions of either over-blown concepts or an onslaught of self-indulgent meanderings. Simple Minds were certainly aware of this; indeed, they shared the same fears. But playing through the tapes, nobody could decide just what should be

scrapped and what should be retained.

"We were changing direction during that album," Jim was to explain later. "To try and get everything on to one album would have put the whole thing out of focus. We could have scrapped tracks, but we had spent money on them and we were proud of them. So in the end we talked with Virgin and agreed to put out two albums. It isn't really a double, we just put them together as a kind of gift."

The two discs were repackaged and sold as single sets after a few months in the shops. But although this stressed the band's continued insistence that they were separate entities, there was a continuity running through the records that bound them together regardless of packaging.

"Sons And Fascination" and "Sister Feelings Call" displayed a new, warm and hazy side to Simple Minds. Whereas in the past they had sounded oppressive and threatening the group were now expanding, opening up more. Yet at the same time they lost none of their earlier power; if anything they packed even more punch than before. The length of the tracks – there were just eight on one album, seven on the other – meant the mood could be sustained for considerably longer as well.

"I'm pleased with the set, although I do feel it's a tiny bit one-paced and samey," Jim told *Melody Maker*. "The only thing we were disappointed in was the production at times. Whereas with 'Empires And Dance' there was novelty in the production, 'Sons And Fascination' was much more traditional and we didn't really see that happening. But some of the feeling in it was really good. There was a lot of beauty on those."

As the music became more expressive, so did Kerr's lyrics. The titles – "70 Cities As Love Brings The Fall", "In Trance As Mission", "Careful in Career" – indicated the way in which he was now working. Lyrics had lost any narrative function and, more than ever before, the accent was on conveying moods. "The lyrics are collage," Jim explained to *Sounds*. "I don't sit down and just write songs and verses. I'm constantly writing and adding things, taking lines that have been written over a period of a year and piecing them together.

"One line can be the image of a song, and the rest can be padding. If it came to a lyric sheet, I'd now rather take a line from each song. I'd think you'd get more of a focus. It's becoming

more of a schizophrenic thing. Of course the lyrics are very important but in terms of value and that, I wouldn't care if no-one at all paid any attention. They're all pictures in themselves, every line's a different picture. It's the atmosphere of words. It could be for the sound, or it could be for the meaning, or for the image of the word. They deal with a lot of images and ambiguities." Although, as Jim was to remark on several occasions, some of the songs on the two albums were superficially very lightweight, there was a depth to them which, Charlie told *Sounds*, ". . . some people are just scared of".

Perhaps the most analysed track on the set was "Boys From Brazil". Set against a thunderous backbeat, on the surface the song seemingly dealt with ideas presented in the Ira Levin book of the same name. "It isn't about the book," Jim contradicted, "although that was a starting point. Rather than find a base line like 'Death to the Neo-Nazis' (as did the book), we wanted to be ambiguous. It was just a point, a motivation. It's a game we play, and when it comes to lyrics I think we're too scared to commit ourselves. (But) that song was concerned with seeing, in Britain, that almost total Neo-Nazi romance, which is really dangerous. There are lines in that, like 'Not just a boy that's crying wolf' and 'Someone else is screaming up at our door'. I was really pleased with them. It is a fascination with style."

He later told *Sounds*: "We wrote "Sons" in America but recorded it in Britain when the riots were going on. People said 'Oh this is really unexpected', but we knew it was coming. It had followed us everywhere – the Munich bomb disaster, street riots in Amsterdam, Italy, Belgium. It just goes to show the attitude of people here who are content to think they're the centre of the world.

"My eyes hit on things and I have to say them. I thought America was all 4th Ave. and Cadillacs but when we were there it was a really anxious time; the hostages had just been released, the key word was heroes. But those people weren't heroes, they were just victims of circumstance who had survived.

"(On another occasion) a newsflash came on saying Reagan had been shot. I jumped out of bed, put on some clothes and dashed down to the bar to get some drinks. And there were all these

Italians there, cheering and celebrating because they thought he'd been bumped off. It would have made a brilliant film . . . I can't let situations like that go to waste."

Perhaps because of the 'limited edition' aspect of the album's initial presentation, perhaps because the two discs showed Simple Minds to have finally come to terms with both their own ambitions and those of their audience, "Sons And Fascination"/"Sister Feelings Call" gave the band their first ever Top 20 LP. It came into the chart at number 14, and eventually rose to number 11. It also supplied them with three consecutive hit singles. "Sweat In Bullet" and "Love Song" were both culled from "Sons And Fascination"; "The American" was one of the highlights of "Sister Feelings Call".

But this sudden acceptance by a mass market did not mean that Simple Minds had finally been drawn into rock's mainstream. In

a year when the biggest selling singles came from the likes of Joe Dolce and The Tweets, when Adam And The Ants seemed poised to monopolise the chart for the rest of the decade, and when the country was only beginning to recover from the narcissistic excesses of the New Romantics, Simple Minds' gently crafted visions of light and shade seemed somehow out of place. They were staunch outsiders in a day and age when an inordinate amount of bands were getting by simply on the strength of particular fashions. And they were rightly proud of the fact. "We're packing out big halls, but we haven't had to cheapen our music to get vital airplay," Jim boasted to *Melody Maker*. "We haven't had to do arrangements we didn't want to, we haven't had to attach ourselves to any category or movement simply because it is currently fashionable. We're still really vulnerable. We dislike people who don't like our music, but we don't believe people

who really do like it. We want to know why they like it."

Of the two albums, "Sister Feelings Call" was the hardest hitting. Despite its containing two very lengthy instrumentals – "Theme For Great Cities" and a vocal-less version of the companion set's "70 Cities As Love Brings The Fall" – the album was built on a solid rock foundation that was absent from much of "Sons And Fascination". On both sets the rhythm tracks were placed well to the forefront. But "Sons And Fascination" used them hypnotically, relentlessly building up to a series of peaks. "Sister Feelings Call" was more dance orientated with a harsh percussive beat which would not have been out of place on "Empires And Dance".

Quite how much emphasis can be placed on Hillage's influence is hard to say. Charlie claimed that although the producer may have introduced ideas and technology with which the band was not familiar, the sound in the final analysis was "a question of character". Hillage's personality was nevertheless stamped indelibly across the proceedings. A short burst of guitar at the end of "The American", for instance, was so highly stylised that, if Hillage didn't play it himself, he at least showed Charlie where to place his fingers.

Other influences, or people whose interest in the band had assisted Simple Minds in the past, were named on the album's back cover. Peter Gabriel was included, so was Rusty Egan, a one-time member of The Rich Kids and now a prominent figure on the London club scene. "He isn't on the album," Jim assured *ZigZag*. "But he's been playing our music in the clubs for about two years now and he's done a lot for us. A lot of people that have heard of us have done so because of the clubs." Ken Lockie, who was a featured backing vocalist on several tracks, was also paid in full for his services. Jim appears in a similar role on Lockie's 1981 album "The Impossible".

As Jim was to say on several occasions, the two albums marked the end of an era for Simple Minds, a twin peak of achievement which finally coalesced the promise and potential of earlier efforts. With "Life In A Day", Simple Minds had been raw and confused. Jim told *Record Mirror*: "We were a band with some

good ideas who had never really been able to break above the heroes that were above us. It was cleaning out all the influences."

"Real To Real Cacophony" was a reaction against "Life In A Day". From having their fingers in every pie, they now had them in none. They went in to record the album with just one song written. Everything, Brian McGee says was pure chance. "Nothing was premeditated because we had nothing to worry about."

The mutant disco of "Empires and Dance" saw the band back on course once again. Their music was still a conditioned response to external influences; the only difference was the band now simply deflecting stimulus rather than attempting to either reflect or absorb it as they had in the past. With "Sons And Fascination"/ "Sister Feelings Call" they continued within that framework, only now they had a far more secure home base – Virgin – from which to work.

1981 saw Simple Minds make further progress in Europe. But perhaps the year's most important moment came in the autumn when they made their first trip to Australia. Virgin had already seen XTC and Magazine make terrific inroads Down Under and were anxious for Simple Minds to complete the trilogy. An

exchange trip was set up whereby Simple Minds would support native superstars Icehouse in Australia, then reverse the billing for a British outing. Icehouse was just one of several bands Simple Minds encountered while they were in Australia, and the experience was, to Charlie, something of a revelation. "Before we went there I thought Australia was going to be really bland," he confessed to *Sounds*. "It's actually a lot more creative than people realise. Sydney's probably going to be the next Hollywood . . ."

Simple Minds also played a string of Australian dates on their own, and found the crowds who had greeted them so enthusiastically on the Icehouse tour were more than happy to return for a second helping. Local independent radio stations took the band to their hearts as well. Before the year was out Simple Minds had made the Aussie top ten with "Love Song". The album and two other singles were substantial hits as well. American sales were promising, Europe was all but sewn up, and even Britain looked ready to succumb at last. Simple Minds faced the new year with more confidence than they had ever felt before.

6

GLITTERING

PRIZE

"Sons And Fascination" was still warm on the tapes when drummer Brian McGee announced his intention to leave the band. It came at a time when Simple Minds' future could have gone in either of two directions; the promise of the new album could be fulfilled with a big hit, or might make a brief appearance low in the chart and be seen no more. Whatever happened the band would be putting in a lot of hard work, touring around the world, and Brian had had enough.

Even in the earliest days Brian had never been totally happy about making music his career. For a start he hated travelling, especially when it meant being away from Glasgow for long periods of time. On top of that he had recently married, and was not at all willing to leave his wife at home while he went gallivanting off round the world with Simple Minds.

The split was quite amicable, and Brian returned to Glasgow where he joined Endgames, an endemic outfit who had supported Simple Minds on several occasions in the past. The band never threatened to set the world on fire, and they remain comfortably second division. Their solitary album to date satisfied a need within Endgames' own loyal following; that the band never seem likely to break into the big league

probably suited Brian when he joined.

For the tours which followed the album's release Simple Minds turned to an old friend from their days at Zoom, Kenny Hyslop. Since The Zones broke up, just before Christmas 1979, he and bassist Russell Webb had been working with The Skids, their arrival prompting Richard Jobson to say: "It's like a perfect group now" The band did not live up to his predictions however, the vocalist's attention turning to loftier art-forms than rock and roll. Said Charlie Burchill of Jobson's new preoccupations: "If you went to see The Skids you'd get all these guys in the audience shouting for 'Albert Tatlock' and Jobson would come out with something like that 'Dulce Et Decorum Est' instead. One minute (he's) Nicky Tesco, the next minute he's Jean-Paul Sartre."

Hyslop joined Simple Minds in August, unharmed by his recent experiences. But his recruitment was never intended to be a permanent arrangement, as Jim informed *ZigZag*. "He hasn't actually joined us. We like him a lot but he's got his fingers in lots of different pies. I don't think we will try and get a permanent drummer. Brian was the only drummer I've ever played with . . . it'll be hard for (anyone) coming

in new and it'd be hard for us as well because we're used to each other, our sense of humour. I think we'll just leave it until the touring's over and see what happens."

The new arrangement actually lasted long enough for Hyslop to play on Simple Minds' new single, the pop orientated "Promised You A Miracle". The band had booked a studio

for ten days in January, intending merely to rehearse. They spent their time making cassettes of riffs and ideas until, according to Jim: "We played 'Promise You A Miracle' for about an hour, thought it sounded good, then went on to something else. But later that night it was going round and round in our heads so we thought we'd just do it, not get precious about it, just see what happened."

Simple Minds thus found themselves with a *bona fide* hit single. It was their ninth attempt. The record entered the charts at the beginning of April, climbing so slowly at first that most people were expecting it to perform the usual stunt of sticking doggedly to the bottom 30. But by the beginning of May it was number 19, a week after that number 15, and seven days later number 13. And although the song's progress was arrested there, the trappings of stardom continued. In the wake of their *Top Of The Pops* appearance, just as the record reached the Top 20, the teenybop magazines turned their beady little eyes towards this new Scottish phenomenon. They have remained by the group's side ever since, charting their progress, their prejudices, and their preferences.

It all caught Simple Minds quite un-

awares. Talking to *Sounds*, Charlie commented; "We've never thought about hit singles until very recently. That's because we feel capable of it now. We didn't form the band to have hit singles and gold albums. We wanted to find a sound with an international appeal. At Arista I thought we were really doomed to be a cult. I believed all that press about us being cold/bleak/industrial. That bothered us because we were making music that deserved to be heard."

In another interview, this time with *Record Mirror*, Jim theorised about why "Promised You A Miracle" had been the one to finally lift Simple Minds out of the cult league which Charlie described. "I think that before, when you heard our singles on the radio, they sounded jarring. They didn't really feel at home. They sounded fine in discos, but radio . . . When I heard 'Promised You A Miracle' on the radio, I burst out grinning!" Later, he was to joke: "If you had asked me last year what somebody who wrote a hit single was like I'd definitely have said they have weird ears.

"If we had tried to write a hit single consciously we really would have missed the point. Some people, like the guys in B.E.F. (Heaven 17) for example, know structure and know what the man in the street wants to hear. They know the right word for the right chord. They know that if you only had two more dBs on that snare you'd have sold 20,000 more in Finland or something. They're students of pop. We've never really studied it."

Kenny Hyslop departed after the single;

when Simple Minds next gathered in the studio, Mike Ogletree, ex-Café Jacques, was in the drum seat. But he was to last for only three numbers: "Somebody Up There Likes You", "New Gold Dream", and the decoratively titled "Colours Fly And Catherine Wheel". The album was completed with Mel Gaynor and, despite Jim's qualms about bringing in a permanent drummer, the exuberant South Londoner has remained with the band ever since. "I seem to be fitting in perfectly," Mel said at the time. "The day I stepped into the studio I found they had a

completely different approach to music. They changed my whole attitude."

Mel's attitude had, in fact, been very different to that of the rest of the band. Apart from a short-lived stint in the engine room of heavy metallurgists Samson, Mel's musical apprenticeship revolved exclusively around British funk music. He had played with Linx, Gonzales and Light Of The World before joining Simple Minds and it was this experience which was to profoundly affect the band. Mel's arrival gave the group more scope, propelling them along in a way Brian McGee never had. Small wonder that Jim was to boast proudly: "We've got a better bass and drum section now than any funk band in Britain, and a guitarist and keyboard player who could play on Genesis or Roxy Music albums."

With the new album slowly beginning to take shape Simple Minds unleashed a second single from the sessions in August. "Glittering Prize" was more assertive than its predecessor, although the strident chorus which had so characterised "Promise You A Miracle" was noticeably absent. The song had a relentless and dreamy quality which caught the imagination of enough people to again push the band into the Top 20.

"Glittering Prize" fell slightly short of the mark made by "Promised You a Miracle", coming to rest at number 16, but Simple Minds were not worrying about the slight drop. When Jim had said earlier in the year that he'd rather be number 13 for five years than number 1 for 6 months, he was speaking for the group as a whole. They had not come this far to be panicked into suddenly becoming a fashionable pop group. When he spoke to *Sounds* in April, Jim expressed the quiet conviction that: ". . . it's time for a dark-horse. There's Human League, Soft Cell, Haircut 100, we can be as bouncy and boyish as any of them but we've also got an undercurrent that we're proud of. There hasn't been a young band with an undercurrent since . . . well The Doors could be AOR, they had different *sides*. The Velvet Underground as well. Loads of other bands were influenced by different *sides* of those bands. You don't get that nowadays but I think we could be the ones, we could win through."

The new régime of confidence, the belief

that they really could win through, stemmed almost exclusively from the music which made up the band's new record. Said Charlie: "Our LPs have been projects in a way and this one felt like us putting together songs which had already been verified as classics."

"New Gold Dream (81-82-83-84)" appeared in the shops in September, and it looked impressive sitting in a sales rack. The sleeve design had heraldic overtones with its

the countdown was nothing of the sort. "We're not afraid to look forward to the future," Jim asserted. "That is just stating the case."

"This is a real transitional period for us", he told *Sounds* shortly before the album's completion. "I've been writing a lot as always, but it is not so much names and places now. It would be a joke to take that further. The story begins with 'I Travel' and finishes with 'Seeing Out The Angel'. I wouldn't want to be the travel

medieval script and a large cross on a marbled background. "I like the image," Jim said of the cross. "It pleases me. I used to wear a Communist hammer and sickle, but not because I'm a Communist or anything. I simply like the shape."

The reference to 1984 in the album's sub-title had no special significance either. Ever since George Orwell first wrote his nightmare vision of a world repressed by a totalitarian régime, and reversed that year's date for its title, the fourth year of the 1980's has been viewed with trepidation, as if Orwell's tale was a concrete prediction. The closer the date became, the louder the clamour to make the ultimate artistic statement on the subject. But for Simple Minds

correspondent of western music or for people to know what to expect from a Simple Minds album."

Simple Minds had been through their experimental phase, he continued. Now they wanted to make an album where every song ". . . is a really focused piece, really up front. The sound will be a lot more obvious but it's the feeling that's changed."

The man selected to see the band through this new era was Peter Walsh. The name was unlikely to ring bells with many people, but Walsh was already well known as a studio engineer. When Steve Lillywhite, Simple Minds' first choice for a producer, proved unable to fit them into his schedule, the band turned to

Walsh. "He's really good," Jim declared in a *New Musical Express* interview. "We put so much in and he takes it out again. But the effect isn't less, it's more."

Unfortunately, as Jim later admitted to *Melody Maker*, Walsh's lack of experience did backfire a little. "Peter never made the band go in a way we didn't want to, but he picked up one side of us as opposed to a kind of overallness. When you hear 'New Gold Dream' live, the tracks go WHOOSH. As for the album, I dunno. There's a lot of good things been said about it and I like that. But other people say it's ethereal mush and that doesn't upset me either."

Around the same time he was to say to the *New Musical Express*: "I was really pleased that we managed to break through and hadn't lost ourselves. We hadn't brought on any star producer who had an arm-load of hits behind him, because we felt that we'd come so far and

then put it into the lap of someone else."

It was easy to construe Jim's meaning. For all Walsh's failings – and to be honest, it was the band's perfectionism, rather than any defects on their producer's behalf, which led to their dissatisfaction with the album – he had captured the essence of the band *at that time* almost perfectly. They could have brought in Steve Lillywhite, or any other big name producer come to that, but they didn't, and when "New Gold Dream" was complete, it was plain they hadn't needed to. Between Walsh and themselves, Simple Minds had finally given their music the clarity of vision which it had lacked in the past. Jim has always been fond of referring to himself as a camera, focusing in on events and emotions, and capturing them in an instant. If that is so, the photography of "New Gold Dream" was as different from earlier albums as Pentax portraits are from box Brownie holiday snaps. "Our records, they're brimful of the date we recorded them," said Kerr. "I just always want to make a music that's in synch with the time it is made."

The visual aspect of the songs was carried across not only in the lyrics but in the music as well. Lynn Hanna, in *New Musical Express*, described "New Gold Dream" as a "series of mini-soundtracks". Jim reacted with delight. "I really do love films, that's the connection. The feeling I can get from listening to a particular track, I can also get from looking at a scene in a film."

It was strange that with this fascination with film Simple Minds did not become more deeply involved in making videos. At a time when Duran Duran were jetting off to exotic locations, Adam Ant was recreating his pantomime fantasies, and Soft Cell were deliberately making dirty little films for dirty little men, Simple Minds would be filmed simply as themselves; playing, walking, standing stock still. They would certainly win no awards for creativity here. But in refusing to glamorise themselves, the band was retaining the honesty which has characterised every move they have made. If they had to make videos, they seemed to be saying, they would make them on their own terms.

There was no fantasy world play acting, no soft focus close-ups, and no hours spent putting on make-up. Just as the band's music

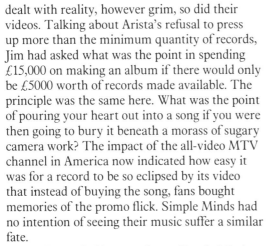

dealt with reality, however grim, so did their videos. Talking about Arista's refusal to press up more than the minimum quantity of records, Jim had asked what was the point in spending £15,000 on making an album if there would only be £5000 worth of records made available. The principle was the same here. What was the point of pouring your heart out into a song if you were then going to bury it beneath a morass of sugary camera work? The impact of the all-video MTV channel in America now indicated how easy it was for a record to be so eclipsed by its video that instead of buying the song, fans bought memories of the promo flick. Simple Minds had no intention of seeing their music suffer a similar fate.

"New Gold Dream" saw Simple Minds make other, equally unusual, departures from standard rock and roll practices. On all the previous albums the writing credits had been divided up so everyone knew who wrote the lyrics (Jim), who wrote the music (Charlie on the first album, the band as a whole on subsequent ones). The songs on "New Gold Dream" were credited solely to Simple Minds for the first time with no individual credits whatsoever. The reasons were purely down to Jim. Although he continued to write all the lyrics, he now explained: "I used to need that egotism. I used to feel insecure because I didn't play any instrument. But now I'm totally satisfied with being part of a five piece band." He did maintain that writing was still ". . . my little piece, it makes me feel I've got something to do," but the need to combat insecurity was no longer there.

The move indicated more than simply one person's feelings however. It proved there was a genuine unity in the band, one that few other groups could honestly claim to possess. With any other band, whether they attempt to

establish their individual personalities or not, it is always the singer, the front man, who gets singled out as both spokesman and leader. It was precisely this which caused so much resentment within the ranks of the early Rolling Stones; guitarist Brian Jones continually seeing himself involved in a struggle for supremacy with Mick Jagger.

Yet Jim happily relinquished his own claim to individual glory, just as in an earlier interview with *ZigZag* he had actually drawn attention to his own limitations. "I don't like to get into the technical, music wise, side," he said. "That's Derek's idea. The way I see it, Derek and the drummer are the feet of the band, Mick and Charlie are the head, and I'm the heart." He

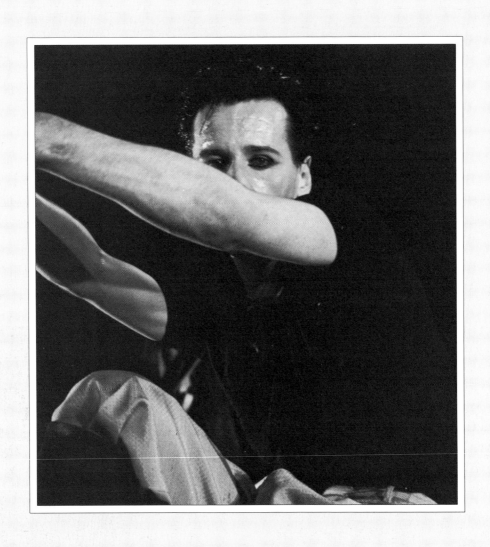

was, of course, also the mouth. At interviews, Derek and Mick would sit so quietly in the background that it was very easy to forget they were there. During one interview, with *Record Mirror*, Derek actually fell asleep! Charlie was more alert, throwing in the occasional sentence or two. Jim, however, would be permanently on the go, pouring out a stream of information, convictions, thoughts and ideas. "I think about the band all the time," he insists. "So when it comes to an opinion being asked, I've always got an answer and I get it out first."

"New Gold Dream" reached number 3 in the charts, compounding the impression that, despite the recent triumph of their singles, Simple Minds was still regarded primarily as an album band. A third single from the set, "Someone, Somewhere, In Summertime", could only scrape in the Top 40.

Later in the new year a *fourth* reissue of

"I Travel' could not even muster the energy to chart at all, prompting observers to wonder just whom the single had been aimed at. Surely anybody who wanted the song would already have "Empires And Dance" which, like the two earlier albums, was still readily available, Virgin having bought the rights to all three from Arista around the same time as "New Gold Dream" was peaking.

The traditional machinations of the business raised their head again. Many record companies faced with a band who look like breaking very big, very soon, buy (or at least attempt to buy) any recordings the artist might have made for other labels. This negates the danger of earlier records suddenly being reactivated in direct competition to official product, and also gives the band stricter control over what is released under their name. In 1972, for example, RCA acquired the rights to several

of David Bowie's previous albums, despite the fact he had only two recent hits to his name. Fifteen years earlier, the same company picked up the first tapes laid down by Elvis Presley.

Simple Minds had already suffered from the attentions of back catalogue compilers. In February 1982, with "Sons And Fascination" having only just dropped out of the chart, Arista put together "Celebration", a potpourri of tracks taken from the band's first three albums. It made the lower regions of the Top 50, and while its success came during a lull in Simple Minds' current recording career and did, in fact, serve to keep their name in the public eye a little longer, there was nothing to stop Arista doing the same thing again at a more dangerous time.

Because the Arista albums had never been deleted, there was no need for Virgin to advertise the repressings with much fanfare. It was considered sufficient that the records

remained available for anyone who wanted them. The label's promotional department was not idle, however, and in a fit of loquaciousness, which far surpassed standard efforts, the initial advertising for "New Gold Dream" claimed the album ". . . conjures up a lushness and depth often lacking in today's music. Simple Minds make music that is thick, layered, twisting, golden and, at the same time, danceable and listenable."

Such ornamental hyperbole is, of course, all part and parcel of the music business. But it is rare that such glowing lines ring so true as these. From the funk groove of "Colours Fly And Catherine Wheel" to the yearningly anthemic "Someone, Somewhere In Summertime", Simple Minds created an album that was little short of majestic. Yet the pomposity, which is usually so vital an ingredient if an album is to be labelled "classic", was absent. Simple Minds' feet remained planted firmly on the ground. Their hopes may have been high, but their expectations were not. When Charlie described "New Gold Dream" as being an album jammed full of classics, the immodesty in his words reflected a calm sense of genuine achievement. Even later, after "New Gold Dream" had given Simple Minds their first ever British gold disc, Jim was to tell *New Musical Express*: "We're still outsiders. The single ('Glittering Prize') dropped this week, so it's not like we're ABC or Duran Duran or the League who can just command. It's just greed and panic to think that we should be up there because we've done this and we've done that."

It was the same sense of continually having to struggle, the knowledge that they could never sit back and relax, whatever happened, which ran through "New Gold Dream". Simple Minds knew that they were making a truly remarkable album, but the idea of allowing that knowledge to become complacency simply never occurred to them.

It was this honesty which gave the album its character, just as it was the very diversity of individual tracks which established an overall sense of continuity. Taken as a whole, "New Gold Dream" was warm and seductive. It was only when you peered beneath the surface, and inspected the songs singularly, that they became as harshly uncompromising as anything Simple

Minds had done in the past. "The King Is White And In The Crowd", the album's reassuringly hypnotic finale, for instance, had been inspired by the assassination of President Sadat. But you had to inhale very deeply before the song's aroma of Middle Eastern mystery became tinged with the stench of cordite. Jim later described "New Gold Dream" as ". . . a coffee table album, a nice thing to have in your home. But I don't think there have been many albums where you've got the coffee table on the surface, but there are worms in the wood underneath. Our next album will be one of the worms."

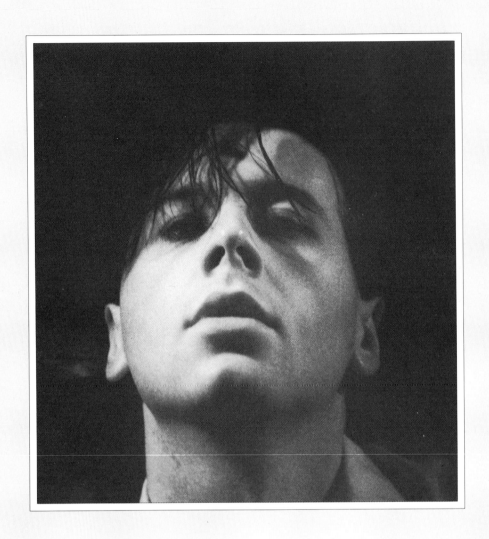

ONE FOR THE
WORMS

"It's hard to know where our destination lies, because we never planned anything from the start," Jim told *Melody Maker*. "We can't really remember saying 'let's make a band', and if you ask any of us what's our ambition I don't think anybody would really know.

"I suppose when I say success I'd really like to do something great. I don't think we've done anything great yet. We used to believe we were going to be a small band, we'd maybe acquire a bit of hipness or something, but now I can see us becoming much more of a force."

Three years into the 1980's the nation's tastemakers were awaiting the advent of a new movement as potent as the Glam and Punk explosions of the previous decade. The Beau Monde of the New Romantics, which had burned so brightly at the turn of the Seventies had changed – or lost – direction, taking with it

the much touted computer age which was to have been *the* sound of the Eighties. A Mod renaissance had gone much the same way, leaving even less of a legacy. The new decade still lay as fallow as the day it first appeared on contemporary calendars.

So, in the absence of a real sense of community amongst the leading bands of the day, it became necessary to invent one. Groups like Depêche Mode, Duran Duran and Spandau Ballet could be linked together through their collective roots in electric dance music. But others, like U2, Echo And The Bunnymen and Simple Minds, remained blissfully unattached.

On the surface, and indeed below it, there seemed little connection between the three bands beyond the fact that their music was, perhaps, less instantly trite and disposable than that of their fellow chart contenders. They were, as one critic so eloquently proclaimed: ". . . intellectual. Not in the way that Eno is intellectual, not even in the way that Paul Weller is intellectual. But in as much as their records provoke serious thought and comment (or are at least intended to), they spearhead a new vanguard of expanded consciousness which far surpasses the meanderings of Spandau, Wham! and all the other sillies who wear their haircuts on their sleeves and their birthdates in *Smash Hits*."

Musically the links were even more tenuous. Ireland's U2 was a hard hitting outfit whose guitar anthems were superficially more suited to football terraces than academic debates. The Bunnymen, from Liverpool, were quiet introverts whose bedsitter image was a total contrast to U2's rabble rousing noise. And Simple Minds were another proposition entirely.

Yet the connection had been made, and with it came a rivalry which, at least for head Bunnyman Ian McCulloch, transcended mere musical terms and became a very one-sided war of words. "We (make) music to compete with Shakespeare, Bosch and Van Gogh," he bragged to *Sounds*. "Not Jim Kerr and Boy George. If Jim Morrison had looked like Jim Kerr he'd still be alive. I wouldn't have thought any band could make it with a singer who looks like W.C. Fields."

Jim and U2's Bono (described by McCulloch as needing "a colostomy bag for

his mouth") preferred to keep a lower profile but were no less outspoken in their own way. "We are without doubt one of the best bands in Britain right now if not in the world," Jim proclaimed. "In the old days we used to keep praising our influences. We don't need to do that now. We don't feel beneath anybody." He countered McCulloch's railery in describing him as insecure. Bono, on the other hand, ". . . is the one person I have the most respect for, in music." The two shared the stage together, performing a duet, when U2 and Simple Minds were billed together at the Belgian Werchter festival in 1983; in Glasgow, 18 months later, Bono joined Simple Minds for an encore of "New Gold Dream" which incorporated snatches from "Take Me To The River", "Light My Fire" and U2's own "I Will Follow" and "Fire".

Simple Minds spent much of 1982-3 on the road, generally concentrating on their fast growing overseas market. Talking to the *New Musical Express*, Jim remembered ". . . that crazy period at the end of the 70's (when) it was embarrassing apparently just to be in a band who made records and toured. All sorts of terms came up, from rockist to people forming their own little limited companies. Touring was out and playing was out. There seemed to be so much talk.

"We've always wanted to be as modern as tomorrow, but in doing that we're one of the most traditional bands out, in as much as we play and make records." Simple Minds, he continued, enjoyed making albums, playing concerts, getting wrecked, all the same things that bands have been doing since time immemorial. "That isn't because we don't have the capacity to think about other things, like playing art galleries and milk bars, those other phases that other bands went through, (because that's) something that has very limited planning and a lot of grind."

Talking to *Sounds*, Charlie added: "Some people think we should take a stance against the routine of recording an album then having to tour to break the album and going through the whole process for eight months then recording again. But I don't know what else we could desire."

"Most bands you see, they're not playing live because they just fucking can't," added Jim. "I still think there's nothing better than if you get a brilliant band in a big hall with a lot of people."

This particular brilliant band was now headlining big halls everywhere; in Canada, Australia, Europe and America. And everywhere the reaction was the same. In December Jim could proudly inform *Sounds* that Simple Minds' then current British tour was, along with similar outings by U2 and Japan, the only one consistently attracting capacity audiences. Even Culture Club, whose "Time" single was in the Top 5, were struggling to make ends meet. "They played in Edinburgh to just 700 people," Jim gloated. In his estimation, too many bands were now coming straight out of nowhere with million selling hits, then taking the 'show' on the road without any experience of live work on which to fall back. ". . . (It) costs six quid (and) people are saying it better be fucking *great* for this money, they go and see it and maybe it's just *alright*.

"When we started this tour, at the first soundcheck I heard the sound and knew the show was going to be absolutely brilliant. It looked great on stage with the lights and everything. I knew we were going to play well, and the support band were China Crisis (just celebrating their first hit single, "African And White") and all for three quid or three-fifty. All that's got to do with why it's selling out."

In November Simple Minds released their irst single in exactly twelve months, the brash "Waterfront". It was as close to rock'n'roll as Simple Minds had ever been and could, perhaps, even be seen as the band's reply to the odious U2 comparisons. They were even using U2 producer Steve Lillywhite, his diary finally corresponding with their own.

This time around Lillywhite was actually the band's second choice. Jim told *Sounds*: "We actually wanted to use Alex Sadkin. We liked the stuff he'd done with Bob Marley and Grace Jones. You could see his face light up when he heard us play. He agreed to do it but then he went off and did Duran Duran, Classix Nouveaux and The Thompson Twins and we thought 'What's going on here?' It just fell apart."

So Lillywhite it was, and the difference he made to the band's studio sound was phenomenal. For the first time the band's live sound had been captured in all its exhilarating glory, and much of the credit for this went to Lillywhite. "He brought out all the energy we normally reserve for interviews or concerts; and we knew beforehand if anybody was able to do that it was him," said Kerr. "You can actually hear Charlie's guitar on this record and, on the new album, you can hear the words on a few tracks. On 'Waterfront' I remember when Derek came in with the bass line it could've been Status Quo."

The tours which followed the release of "New Gold Dream" kept the band on the road for six months. Jim told *Melody Maker*: "We came back and wrote these new songs, feeling very chuffed and smug. But a week later we found out all we were doing was writing "New Gold Dream" part 2, which was really awful. It was a

big problem at the beginning of the year. I was drying up. At least everything I wrote seemed to be either the same as "New Gold Dream", or a parody of it. Which is why there hasn't been an album all year, because this mental block came on."

It took a trip home, to Glasgow, to break the block. "I went for a walk one night and ended up literally on the banks of the Clyde. I went right to where the town ends to what were once the shipyards. It was eerie. All I could hear were my own footsteps and I was surrounded by factories which are just shells now.

"I just started to think what it was like in its day. Some of my people, my grandfather and stuff, had worked there. There was a predominant bleakness but the great thing was being able to see the water. It was still moving and it seemed to hold some kind of symbol, because it was there when the city was first built and it'll still be there when the city goes. It's not being romantic but . . . I still believe things will turn round and life will go back there and strength will still come from there. It just made me write a few simple words, just a verse, an anecdote even, which happened to fit a backing track that came up. There was no European in it, no president getting shot, no fugitives, but it was important for me and for anyone listening to the song. I'm confident they can feel uplifted, because that's how I felt at the time."

"Waterfront", backed by a version of "Hunter And The Hunted", recorded live in Newcastle the previous year, returned Simple Minds to the chart almost instantly. It also became their biggest hit to date, an omen that boded well for the release of their new album set for early in the new year. The annual poll results published in the music papers were no less encouraging. Individually and collectively Simple Minds scooped places in almost every category for which they were eligible.

The album finally arrived at the end of February, hot on the heels of another hit, the explosive "Speed Your Love To Me". It smashed straight into the chart at number one, as triumphant an accomplishment as the music contained within the sleeve. From the opening crashes of "Up On The Catwalk", through to the grand finale, "Shake Off The Ghosts", the album was one big, joyous celebration. Jim

referred to the album as, ". . . manic I don't know how we went from 'New Gold Dream' to that, but we did. One track, 'Kick Inside Of Me' sounded like a Sex Pistols track!" Derek added; "My fingers were physically bleeding from the track. I just went mad."

The sheer energy of the album was a revelation; every song a sharp rebuke for anyone who ever accused Simple Minds of stodginess, of being boring. Even when they slowed the pace down, as on the moody "White Hot Day", there was a latent strength in the sound which could rival the most demented powerhouse band.

On "New Gold Dream," Jim explained, the band were, ". . . obsessed with a pursuit of perfection. "And 'New Gold Dream' was obsessed with a quiet power. But this album hasn't got any time for dreaminess, it's really straight for the jugular.

"Our rock is dead hard – it hasn't got rock clichés but rock dynamism. We're going for the giant sound . . ."

The group also recorded a cover version for the first time. In concert they had frequently encored with rousing assaults on "Vicious", "White Light/White Heat" and "Waiting For The Man", songs written by Lou Reed (despite Jim's occasional habit of introducing the latter as the work of another of Simple Minds' heroes, Richard Strange). This time it was Reed's epic "Street Hassle" which came in for a revival.

"Street Hassle" was not, on first glance, a song which anyone could have covered with ease, let alone with success. But in severely truncating Reed's original twelve minute masterpiece, and by restructuring the lyrics, Simple Minds achieved both. And while purists might have complained about the deletion of several verses from Reed's original, the composer himself had done very little in recent years to justify any such consideration. His albums since 1973's love/hate/death cycle, "Berlin", had been patchy affairs notable more for the number of sow's ears than silk purses they contained.

1979's "Street Hassle", however, gave Reed an artistic renaissance. He had recently joined a new record company (ironically, it was Arista) and while that label had proved ultimately stifling to Simple Minds, it regenerated Reed to the extent that many critics described "Street Hassle" (his second album for

the label) as his finest work since The Velvet Underground.

The title track was singled out for particular praise. Its simple melody was hammered home through mesmerising repetition, Reed solemnly intoning three stories over it. The first focused in on two strangers meeting in a bar. In the second, the only one which Simple Minds used, they make love. In the third, the girl overdoses at a party. Reed's treatment of these scenarios is a masterpiece of spoken irony and disdain; he calls up love and then despatches it as violently as he ever did with The Velvets. It was a painful song to hear, and a courageous step for Simple Minds to take. But take it they did, and for many people their version was one of "Sparkle In The Rain's" most evocative moments.

It was, perhaps, predictable that "Sparkle In The Rain" would suffer at the hands of the music press. Critics who five years before had looked on with horror at the overkill which surrounded Simple Minds' launch were now to be found yearning for those days when the group had been a jealously guarded secret, a band to be savoured in the privacy of one's own home or in a sweaty club with a few hundred other, similar converts. People who had written the group off as being derivative, old fashioned, and utterly disposable, now sang the praises of the very albums they had once hammered and hated. It was typical rock press behaviour, the kind that insists a group is always worse now than in earlier days. Simple Minds used to have something to say, the critics mourned. Now they are just shallow and hollow; all Steve Lillywhite had done was make empty garbage sound grand and meaningful.

"All that is just crap," Jim snarled angrily. "We could have written those reviews; in fact, we did write them. We're dead in control now, and I think that shines through. Review wise, for us there's certain people who dismissed us this time last year and who now go out of their way to say we're crap and will use four or five paragraphs to do it.

"I think a lot of the things I said in interviews last year have annoyed people – just the tone of it. But I think there's a certain glow in my interviews. They're usually picturesque and pretty entertaining, which is more than can be said for the Paul Wellers of this world."

For the "Waterfront" video Simple Minds played a short, free show in Glasgow for the benefit of the cameras and as a thank-you to their fans. As Jim had remarked several years before, the band found home town gigs difficult to arrange. Early dates at the Mars Bar aside, Simple Minds' Glasgow dates were usually confined to the local Tiffany's, the venue for their last show in town at Christmas 1982. This time, though, the band decided to break with tradition; instead of taking over the Apollo or some other converted cinema, the location they chose was Barrowlands' Ballroom.

In the 1960's the venue won itself a very well deserved reputation for violence. Gangland fights were so commonplace that it was unusual not to find half-a-dozen police cars parked outside; if you walked out in as good health as you walked in, you were lucky.

Barrowlands had stood empty for years; now Simple Minds were to reopen it, re-establishing it on the national gig circuit. When they played a short string of dates in London and Glasgow just before Christmas it was Barrowlands which hosted the three Scottish shows. Later still, during their spring tour, the band made four consecutive appearances there, alongside two nights each in Edinburgh, Dublin and Birmingham. The itinerary also included a dozen-plus one-nighters throughout the British Isles and, to climax the outing, an incredible seven shows at London's Hammersmith Odeon.

Jim admitted to *Melody Maker*: "We do go mad when a record comes out, running around and talking. At the end of 1982 I looked at myself and thought I looked like I should be in a band. I'd always denied the danger of being on tour for a year. I always said it would never catch up with us because we had too much energy. But last year when we got back, in one week we got just about everything that means thumbs up from the music industry, be it gold discs, or front pages, or topping a lot of the polls. I'm not saying we're ungrateful bastards but we never felt up or down. I think it was due to total fatigue and being generally knackered. And that's a bit frightening."

Midway through the UK tour, a very unexpected – and unwelcome – excuse to take a break presented itself to the band. For a month

Jim had been soldiering bravely on despite having fallen victim to the latest 'flu bug to be imported from the continent. The ravages of the virus finally overcame him in Birmingham just as the band reached the end of their programmed set. The planned encore was cancelled and Jim was rushed back to the hotel where a doctor demanded he remain for another ten days. The rest of the tour was cancelled forthwith, and Jim lay back to wait out his convalescence.

He bounced back for the band's European tour in April. Then, with a few days to spare before the rescheduled British dates were due to begin, he vanished to New York. There, in a hushed registry office ceremony, he and Pretenders' vocalist Chrissie Hynde shocked gossip columnists the world over by getting married.

Chrissie had, as far as anybody else knew, been living happily with Ray Davies, the resident songwriter/singer/genius in The Kinks. He had fathered Chrissie's daughter, Natasha, and most of the couple's friends were confidently predicting a marriage right up until Chrissie took Jim for her spouse. Several newspapers immediately interpreted Jim's "all the day and all of the night" introduction to "Speed Your Love To Me" as a further slight to Davies. It was, of course, immaterial that the line was actually corrupted from one of the song's verses, and had, therefore, been around a lot longer than the so-called news story.

Simple Minds resumed their British tour a week later, picking up where they had left off, with a show in Birmingham. A night in St. Austell, Cornwall, followed, and then came the Hammersmith dates – now swollen by demand to eight consecutive concerts; a tally which equalled the Odeon's previous record set by Elton John's Christmas 1982 shows. And at the end of it all, with the sound of an enraptured crowd still loud in their ears, and a celebrity packed party at Richard Branson's Canal Club to help the group wind down, even the most cynical observer could not deny that Simple Minds had finally arrived.

Their Christmas, 1984 shows at Barrowlands were sold out before the dates had even been announced by the music press; the three gigs were recorded for a live album which

can only compound what the pundits have already applauded. Simple Minds are one of the most successful bands this country has ever seen. Not, perhaps, in the same way as The Beatles, The Stones, or David Bowie, but even those peaks are in sight. Their music is already as crafted as anything Lennon and McCartney ever did. Their opinions can be as outspoken as any by Mick or Keith. Their live performances are as spectacular, as exciting, as any of David Bowie's. But it has all been accomplished without any of the trappings which normally accompany such success. There have been no scandals, no drug busts, no highly publicised affairs, no internal bust ups. Even as they began the final sprint to their current status, Simple Minds remained firmly, even gleefully, unfashionable. Apart from those few months right at the very start, nobody has ever been able to accuse them of being darlings of the press. And even then, when you only had to glance at the music press to find their name surrounded by superlatives, there was enough world-weary cynicism in the band's own words to make it obvious that not only were they not taking the praise to heart, they weren't even taking it seriously.

Simple Minds' policy has always been one of the utmost simplicity: to make music of which they can be proud and which reflects the knowledge that it all came direct from their own hearts. They have not yet reached that position, they claim, but it comes closer with every record they make and every concert they play. Effortlessly Simple Minds move forward, knowing that one day the pinnacles of perfection which they have sought for so long will be within reach. But until they are, Simple Minds will keep expanding, keep growing, keep challenging. Which is just how it should be.

DISCOGRAPHY

DISCOGRAPHY 1: ALBUMS

LIFE IN A DAY
Someone/Life In a Day/Sad Affair/All For You/Pleasantly Disturbed/No Cure/Chelsea Girl/Wasteland/Destiny/Murder Story
Zoom ZULP 1 Apr. 1979
All songs composed Kerr/Burchill, produced by John Leckie, full colour sleeve with b/w insert, reached no. 30 in chart.

REAL TO REAL CACOPHONY
Real To Real/Naked Eye/Citizen (Dance Of Youth)/Carnival (Shelter In A Suitcase)/Factory/Cacophony/Veldt/Changeling/Premonition/Film Theme/Calling Your Name/Scar
Arista SPART 1109 Nov. 1979
All songs composed Kerr (lyrics)/Simple Minds (music), produced by John Leckie, blue sleeve with silver lettering, b/w photo insert.

EMPIRES AND DANCE
I Travel/Today I Died Again/Celebrate/This Fear Of Gods/Capital City/Constantinople Line/Twist·Run·Repulsion/30 Frames A Second/Kant-Kino/Room
Arista SPART 1140 Sept. 1980
Composed and produced as above, full colour sleeve with b/w photo/lyric insert, first 10,000 copies sold at reduced price, reached no. 41 in chart.

SONS AND FASCINATION
In Trance As Mission/Sweat In Bullet/70 Cities As Love Brings The Fall/Boys From Brazil/Love Song/This Earth That You Walk Upon/Sons And Fascination/Seeing Out The Angel
Virgin V2207 Aug. 1981
Composed/produced as above, full colour sleeve, first 10,000 contained bonus LP, reached no. 11 in chart.

SISTER FEELINGS CALL
Theme For Great Cities/The American/20th Century Promised Land/Wonderful In Young Life/League Of Nations/Careful In Career/Sound In 70 Cities
Virgin OVED 2 Aug. 1981
Composed/produced as above, released separately in blue/white sleeve.

CELEBRATION
Life In A Day/Chelsea Girl/Premonition/Factory/Calling Your Name/I Travel/Changeling/Celebrate/30 Frames A Second/Kaleidoscope
Arista SPART 1183 Feb. 1982
Tracks 1, 2 from LP ZULP 1
Tracks 3, 4, 5, 7 from LP SPART 1109
Tracks 6, 8, 9 from LP SPART 1140
Track 10 from single ARIST 372c
Full colour picture sleeve, reached no. 45 in chart.

NEW GOLD DREAM (81-82-83-84)
Someone, Somewhere In Summertime/Colours Fly And Catherine Wheel/Promised You A Miracle/Big Sleep/Somebody Up There Likes You/New Gold Dream (81-82-83-84)/Glittering Prize/Hunter And The Hunted/King Is White And In The Crowd
Virgin V2230 Sept. 1982
All tracks composed by Simple Minds, produced by Peter Walsh, full colour sleeve with gold insert, reached no. 3 in chart.

LIFE IN A DAY
Tracks as ZULP 1
Virgin VM 6 Oct. 1982

REAL TO REAL CACOPHONY
Tracks as SPART 1109
Virgin V2246 Oct. 1982

EMPIRES AND DANCE
Tracks as SPART 1140
Virgin V2247 Oct. 1982

CELEBRATION
Tracks as SPART 1183
Virgin V2248 Oct. 1982

SPARKLE IN THE RAIN
Up On The Catwalk/Book Of Brilliant Things/Speed Your Love To Me/Waterfront/East At Easter/Street Hassle/White Hot Day/'C' Moon Cry Like A Baby/The Kick Inside Of Me/Shake Off The Ghosts
Virgin V2300 Feb. 1984
All tracks composed by Simple Minds except track 6 by Lou Reed, produced by Steve Lillywhite, full colour sleeve with b/w insert, reached no.1 in chart.

SINGLES

JOHNNY AND THE SELF ABUSERS

Saints And Sinners/Dead Vandals
Chiswick NS22 Nov. 1977
Both songs composed: Kerr/Burchill/McGee/Donald/Milarky/McNeil
Produced by Johnny & The Self Abusers, b/w picture sleeve.

SIMPLE MINDS

Life In A Day/Special View
Zoom ZUM 10 Apr. 1979
A-side from LP ZULP 1, B-side composed/produced as above, black sleeve with red lettering, reached no. 62 in chart.

Chelsea Girl/Garden Of Hate
Zoom ZUM 11 July 1979
A-side from LP ZULP 1, B-side composed/produced as above, full colour sleeve.

Changeling/Premonition
Arista ARIST 325 Nov. 1979
A-side edited from LP SPART 1109, B-side live, Hurrah, New York, 24/10/79. Composed as above. Picture Sleeve.

I Travel/New Warm Skin (single)
Arista ARIST 372 Sept. 1980
A-side from LP SPART 1140, B-side composed/produced as above. Picture sleeve. Initial pressings contained bonus flexidisc pressed on turquoise picture vinyl.

Kaleidoscope/Film Theme Dub (single)
Arista ARIST 372c Sept. 1980
Both composed/produced as above.

I Travel/Film Theme Dub (single)
Arista ARIST 12372 Sept. 1980
A-side from LP SPART 1140, B-side from single ARIST 372c.
12″ single with picture sleeve.

Celebrate/Changeling/I Travel (single)
Arista ARIST 394 Apr. 1981
Tracks 1, 3, from LP SPART 1140.
Track 2 from LP SPART 1109.
Picture sleeve.

Celebrate/Changeling/I Travel (single)
Arista ARIST 12394 Apr. 1981
Tracks 1, 3 from LP SPART 1140.
Track 2 from LP SPART 1109.
12″ single with picture sleeve.

The American/League Of Nations (single)
Virgin VS 410 May 1981
Composed as above, produced by Steve Hillage.
A- and B-sides from LP OVED 2, full colour picture sleeve, reached no. 59 in chart.

The American/League Of Nations
Virgin VS 410-12 May 1981
A-side extended version of track on LP OVED 2, B-side from LP OVED 2, 12″ single with picture sleeve.

Love Song/This Earth That You Walk Upon
Virgin VS 434 Aug. 1981
A- and B-sides from LP V2207, full colour picture sleeve,
reached no. 47 in chart.

Love Song/This Earth That You Walk Upon
Virgin VS 434-12 Aug. 1981
A-side extended version of track on LP V2207, B-side from LP
V2207, 12″ single with picture sleeve.

Sweat In Bullet/20th Century Promised Land
Virgin VS 451 Nov. 1981
A-side remixed from LP V2207 B-side from LP OVED 2, full
colour picture sleeve, initial pressings released in gatefold
sleeve with bonus single, reached no. 52 in chart.

Premonition/In Trance As Mission
Virgin VS 451c Nov. 1981
A- and B-sides recorded live, Odeon Hammersmith Sept. 1981,
Produced by Peter Walsh.

*Sweat In Bullet/20th Century Promised Land/Premonition/
In Trance As Mission*
Track 1 remixed from LP V2207. Track 2 from LP OVED 2.
Tracks 3, 4 recorded live, Odeon Hammersmith, Sept. 1981,
12″ single with picture sleeve.

I Travel/30 Frames A Second
Arista ARIST 448 Jan. 1982
A-side from LP SPART 1109, B-side recorded live, picture sleeve.

I Travel/30 Frames A Second/I Travel
Arista ARIST 12448 Jan. 1982
Track 1 from LP SPART 1109
Tracks 2,3 recorded live
12″ single with picture sleeve.

Promised You A Miracle/Theme For Great Cities
Virgin VS 448 April 1982
A-side from LP V2230, B-side from LP OVED 2, picture sleeve,
reached no. 13 in chart.

*Promised You A Miracle/Theme For Great Cities/Seeing
Out The Angel*
Virgin VS 448-12 April 1982
Track 1 extended version of track on LP V2230
Track 2 as above,
Track 3 instrumental remix of track on LP V2207
12″ single with picture sleeve.

Glittering Prize/Glittering Theme
Virgin VS 511 Aug. 1982
A-side for LP V2230, B-side composed by Simple Minds
produced by Peter Walsh, picture sleeve, reached no. 16 in chart

Glittering Prize/Glittering Theme
Virgin VS 511-12 Aug. 1982
A-side extended version of track on LP V2230, B-side as above,
12″ single with picture sleeve.

*Someone, Somewhere In Summertime/King Is White And
In The Crowd*
Virgin VS 538 Nov. 1982
A-side from LP V2230, B-side from David Jensen/BBC session
11 Feb. 1982, picture sleeve opens into four colour poster, reached
no. 36 in chart.

*Someone, Somewhere In Summertime/King Is White And
In The Crowd/Soundtrack From Every Heaven (single)*
Virgin VS 538-12 Nov. 1982
Tracks 1, 2 as above, track 3 composed/produced as above,
12″ single with picture sleeve.

Waterfront/Hunter And The Hunted (single)
Virgin VS 636 Nov. 1983
A-side from LP V2300, B-side recorded live, Newcastle City
Hall, 21 Nov. 1982, picture sleeve, reached no. 13 in chart.

*Waterfront/Hunter And The Hunted/If You Want My Love
(single)*
Virgin VS 636-12 Nov.1983
Tracks 1, 2 as above, track 3 composed/produced as above
12″ single with picture sleeve.

Speed Your Love To Me/Bass Line (single)
Virgin VS 649 Jan. 1984
A-side from LP V2300, B-side composed/produced as above,
picture sleeve, reached no. 20 in chart.

Speed Your Love To Me/Bass Line (single)
Virgin VS 649-12 Jan. 1984
A-side extended version of track on V2300, B-side as above,
12″ single with picture sleeve.

Up On The Catwalk/Brass Band In Africa
Virgin VS 661 Mar. 1984
A-side from LP V2300, B-side composed/produced as above,
reached no. 27 in chart.

Up On The Catwalk/Brass Band In Africa
Virgin VS 661-12 Mar. 1984
A- and B-sides as above, 12″ single with picture sleeve.

DISCOGRAPHY II: VARIOUS ARTISTS COMPILATIONS

"THE OLD GREY WHISTLE TEST" (LP)
BBC BELP 017 1979
includes "Chelsea Girl", from LP ZULP 1

"MODERN DANCE" (LP)
K-Tel NE 1156 1981
includes "Love Song," "Sweat In Bullet" from LP V2207

"SUPER HITS VOLUME ONE" (LP)
Ronco RTL 2058 1981
includes "Love Song," from LP V2207

"METHODS OF DANCE" (LP)
Virgin OVED 5 1981
includes "Love Song," from LP V2207

"HITS" (LP)
Ronco RTL 2063 1981
includes "Sweat In Bullet", from LP V2207

"OVERLOAD" (LP)
Ronco RTL 2079 1982
includes "Promised You A Miracle", from LP V2230

"MODERN HEROES" (LP)
TV Records TV 1 1982
includes "Promised You A Miracle", from LP V2230

"CHART ATTACK" (LP)
Telstar STAR 2221 1982
includes "Glittering Prize", from LP V2230

"METHODS OF DANCE VOLUME TWO" (LP)
Virgin OVED 7 Nov. 1982
includes "Soundtrack From Every Heaven", from single
VS 538-12

**"NOW THAT'S WHAT I CALL MUSIC VOLUME
ONE" (LP)**
Virgin/EMI NOW 1 Nov. 1983
includes "Waterfront", from LP V2300

DISCOGRAPHY III: SELECTED FOREIGN RELEASES

"CATCH A WAVE" (LP)
C.A.W. Records NICE 102 1977
Scandinavian punk compilation includes "Saints and Sinners", from single NS22

"LIFE IN A DAY" (LP)
PVC Records PVC 7904 1979
American counterpart of UK release, LP ZULP 1

"Life In A Day"/"Special View" (single)
PVC Records 1979
American counterpart of UK release, single ZUM 10

"SIMPLE MINDS"
CBS 241033 1980
Australian double album featuring UK LPs ZULP 1 and SPART 1109

"I Travel"/"Film Theme Dub" (single)
Arista 600 289 Sept. 1980
French counterpart of UK release, single 12372

"THEMES FOR GREAT CITIES" (LP)
Stiff TEES 2 1981
American compilation of tracks from LP V2207 and LP OVED 2 (double album)

"SISTER FEELINGS CALL" (EP)
Virgin VEP 311 1981
Canadian compilation includes; 70 Cities As Love Brings Fall/ Careful In Career/Seeing Out The Angel/Wonderful In Young Life/Sound In 70 Cities. Tracks 1, 3 from LP V2207, tracks 2, 4, 5 from LP OVED 2. Cassette version (VEP4 311) features extra track; "This Earth That You Walk Upon", from LP V2207

"MODERN DANCE" (LP)
K-Tel MD 9018 1981
Scandinavian compilation includes "Theme For Great Cities" From LP OVED 2

"ROCK OF THE EIGHTIES VOLUME THREE" (LP)
Virgin 2473-822 1981
Greek compilation
includes "The American" From LP OVED 2

"I Travel"/"New Gold Dream (81-82-83-84)"
Virgin 600-796-213 1983
European 12″ single, white vinyl, A-side from LP SPART 1140, B-side from LP V2230

"SPARKLE IN THE RAIN"
A&M SP6 4981 1984
American counterpart of UK release Album V2300

DISCOGRAPHY IV: BOOTLEG RECORDS

"THE BEST YEARS OF OUR LIVES" (LP)
Capital City/Here Comes The Fool/Calling Your Name/Life In A Day/Citizen (Dance Of Youth)/Factory/Changeling/ Pleasantly Disturbed/White Light White Heat

Good Shape Records 1980
A very good stereo recording from the Amsterdam Paradico 23 March 1980. "Here Comes The Fool" and Lou Reed's "White Light, White Heat" have never been made available officially

"LIVE IN ITALIA" (LP)
Somebody Up There Likes You/King Is White And In The Crowd/Glittering Prize/I Travel/Colours Fly And Catherine Wheel/Promised You A Miracle/The American/Big Sleep/Love Song
Recorded in Bologna in 1982.

"ART APPEAL" (LP)
King Is White And In The Crowd/Glittering Prize/I Travel/ Celebrate/Hunter And The Hunted/Promised You A Miracle/ New Gold Dream (81-82-83-84)/Love Song
Clean Sound Records N1001
Recorded in Ostia, Italy, March 1983

DISCOGRAPHY V: SELECTED BOOTLEG TAPES

GLASGOW MARS BAR, 30 July 1978
Tonight/Take Me To The Angels/Chelsea Girl/Act Of Love/ Saints And Sinners/Dead Vandals/Murder Story/White Light, White Heat/Caught In A Dream/European Son/Watch Out/ Wasteland/Doobe-b-doo/Cocteau Twins
A very representative selection from Simple Minds' earliest repertoire. Tracks 5, 6 had already appeared as the Johnny And The Self Abusers' single (NS22); tracks 3, 7, 12 were to reappear on the LP ZULP 1. All other songs remain unreleased in any form. Trivia freaks may be interested to know that The Cocteau Twins apparently took their name from this Simple Minds' song.

DEMOS 1978/1979
Act Of Love/Cocteau Twins/Chelsea Girl/Pleasantly Disturbed/ Wasteland/Did You Ever?/Someone/A Special View/Murder Story/Sad Affair/Rosemary's Baby
Tracks 1-6 were recorded at Savva Studios in May 1978. Tracks 7-11 were recorded at the same place in January 1979. Tracks 3, 4, 5, 7, 9, 10 all appear on ZULP 1 in re recorded form. Track 8 became the B-side of ZUM 10

IN CONCERT, 8 Sept. 1979
Live stereo tape from BBC Radio broadcast

LIVE, HURRAH! MANHATTAN, 24 Oct. 1979
LIVE, TIFFANY'S, GLASGOW, 1/3/81
LIVE, THE EDGE, TORONTO, 18/3/81
LIVE, HAMMERSMITH ODEON, LONDON, 9/81
LIVE, KAREN FESTIVAL, SWEDEN, 17/2/82
LIVE, COASTERS, EDINBURGH, 9/9/82
LIVE, CITY HALL, NEWCASTLE, 21/11/82
LIVE, TIFFANY'S, GLASGOW, 21/12/82
LIVE, NIJMEGEN, 7/3/83
LIVE, ROLLING STONE, MILAN, 17/3/83
LIVE, PINK POP FESTIVAL, 23/5/85
LIVE, WERCHTER FESTIVAL, 3/7/83
LIVE, PHOENIX PARK, DUBLIN, 13/8/83
LIVE, LYCEUM, LONDON, 17/12/83
LIVE, NARARA FESTIVAL, Jan. 1984
LIVE, HAMMERSMITH ODEON, LONDON, 12/5/84
LIVE, UP ALL NIGHT, NEW JERSEY, 27/5/84

This is only a very tiny selection of bootleg tapes which are, or have been, available. It is feasible that, if you look hard enough, you will find someone with a tape of any Simple Minds show you care to name. I have heard of several which were recorded during the Magazine tour in 1979; there are also recordings (possibly video) of Simple Minds' appearances on the *Old Grey Whistle Test*, *The Tube*, *Top Of The Pops*, and *Rock Around The Clock '84*.

DISCOGRAPHY VI: MISCELLANEOUS

"SOLDIER" (IGGY POP) (LP)
Arista SPART 1117 1980
The entire band are featured on backing vocals on several tracks, although their only credit is alongside David Bowie on "Play It Safe"

"THE IMPOSSIBLE" (KEN LOCKIE) (LP)
Virgin V2081 1981
Jim Kerr is credited with backing vocals on this album

THE CUBAN HEELS (featuring several former members of Johnny And The Self Abusers) have released the following:
"Downtown"/"Smoke Walk" (single)
Housewives' Choice Records JY 1/2 4/78

"Little Girl"/"Fast Living Friend"
Greville Records GR 1 8/80

"Walk On Water"/"Take A Look" (single)
Cuba Libra Records DRINK 1/81

"WORK OUR WAY TO HEAVEN" (LP)
Cuba Libra Records V2210 10/81
initial pressings contained free magazine

"Walk On Water"/"Hard Times" (single)
Virgin VS 440 /81
initial pressings contained free flexi "Matthew And Son"

"ROCK OF THE EIGHTIES VOLUME THREE" (LP)
Virgin 2473-822 /81
Greek compilation includes "Sweet Charity"
ENDGAMES (featuring Brian McGee)

"BEYOND THE GROOVE" (LP)
101/Polydor 2478 140 1981
Various artists compilation includes "Joy of Life"

"HEAT FROM THE STREET" (LP)
Charisma CLASS 8 1981
Various artists compilation includes one cut – title unknown

"LIVE LETTERS" (LP)
101/Polydor 2478 1981
Various artists compilation includes one cut – title unknown

"Waiting For Another Chance"/"Universe" (single)
Virgin VS 605/60512 6/1983

"Love Cares"/"Ready Or Not" (single)
Virgin VS 617/61712 8/1983

"Miracle Of My Heart"/"Instrumental"/"Ecstasy" (single)*
Virgin VS 640/64012* 11/1983

"BUILDING BEAUTY" (LP)
Virgin V2287 10/1983

"Desire" – (single)
Virgin VS 651 1984

MEL GAYNOR
Prior to joining Simple Minds was a member of LIGHT OF THE WORLD. He also plays, as a session man, on various records by LINX and GONZALES

FEATURED MUSICIANS

On several occasions Simple Minds have recruited outside musicians to help out on sessions.

JACQUI: chorus on V2207

KEN LOCKIE: Chorus on V2207. Own recording career with Virgin Records

SHARON CAMPBELL: voice on V2230, two tracks

HERBIE HANCOCK: solo on V2230, one track. Own recording career with CBS Records

MIKE OGLETREE: drums/percussion on V2230. Formerly with CAFE JACQUES (2 LPs on CBS)

KENNY HYSLOP: drums on V2230, one track. Also singles VS448/448-12 (A-side), VS 538/538-12 (B-side), VS 636/636-12 (B-side) and tours. Formerly with Slik (1 single on Polydor, 4 on Bell, 1 on Arista, 1 LP on Bell), PVC2 (1 single on Zoom), The Zones (1 single on Zoom, 3 on Arista, 1 LP on Arista)

KIRSTY MacColl: Girl's voice on V2300 (two tracks) Own recording career with Stiff Records